DISCOVER THE SHORTEST ROUTE TO "HAPPY, CONFIDENT, IN CONTROL"

Richard Carlson, a renowned California stress-management consultant, has helped thousands of clients cut through the "red tape" of traditional therapy to manage their problems and feel great about life. Now he dares to reveal what most counselors and mental health practitioners won't tell you: you yourself can master the ten essential tools for building mental health that will truly change your life. This extraordinary book offers a direct route to long-term positive changes in the shortest possible time.

"A remarkably reasonable and clear-headed book that will help many people."

—Rabbi Harold Kushner,
author of *When Bad Things Happen to Good People*

Richard Carlson holds a Ph.D. in psychology and operates a stress-management center in Walnut Creek, California. He is a frequent lecturer and the author of five previous books, including *You Can Feel Good Again* (Plume). He lives with his wife and two sons in Northern California.

Richard Carlson, Ph.D.

Shortcut Through Therapy

Ten Principles of Growth-Oriented, Contented Living

A PLUME BOOK

PLUME
Published by the Penguin Group
Penguin Books USA Inc., 375 Hudson Street,
New York, New York 10014, U.S.A.
Penguin Books Ltd, 27 Wrights Lane,
London W8 5TZ, England
Penguin Books Australia Ltd, Ringwood,
Victoria, Australia
Penguin Books Canada Ltd, 10 Alcorn Avenue,
Toronto, Ontario, Canada M4V 3B2
Penguin Books (N.Z.) Ltd, 182–190 Wairau Road
Auckland 10, New Zealand

Penguin Books Ltd, Registered Offices:
Harmondsworth, Middlesex, England

First published by Plume, an imprint of Dutton Signet,
a division of Penguin Books USA Inc.

First Printing, April, 1995
10 9 8 7 6 5 4 3 2 1

Ⓟ REGISTERED TRADEMARK—MARCA REGISTRADA

Library of Congress Cataloging-in-Publication Data

Carlson, Richard.
   Shortcut through therapy : ten principles of growth-oriented, contented living / Richard Carlson.
      p. cm.
   "A Plume book."
   ISBN 0-452-27383-8 : $9.95
   1. Self-actualization (Psychology) 2. Contentment. 3. Behavior modification. I. Title.
BF637.S4C365   1995
158'.1—dc20
                                                              94-35016
                                                              CIP

Printed in the United States of America
Set in New Baskerville
Designed by Leonard Telesca

Contents

Introduction

The greatest discovery of my generation is that a human being can alter his life by altering his attitude.

—WILLIAM JAMES

For more than ten years I have worked successfully with clients, helping them to deal with various issues—stress, relationship problems, anger, job burnout, and frustration. I call myself a stress management professional, but what I actually do is teach people the principles that allow them to regain their emotional bearings. I help them make a shift from a state of distress and frustration to one of relative peace and harmony. Simply put, I teach people how to be happy!

This book distills the most relevant components of my work, the critical inch of what I teach. Through many years of interaction with clients and readers, I have learned what I believe are the ten essential principles for becoming a happier, more growth-oriented person.

The goal of this book is to give you the essence of these principles. They are offered as shortcuts to implementing immediately what you learn. If you master these principles and put them into practice, you won't need traditional therapy. You will have already learned the best of what therapy has to offer.

You can spend any number of years with a therapist. If all goes well, you come away with some useful tools for a better emotional experience of life. You grow as a person and you understand the principles that are most relevant to your personal growth and happiness. Although therapy can help, it's almost always extremely time-consuming and very expensive. This book offers you an alternative to the process of therapy.

> *The shortest distance between any two points is a straight line, and this book is the straight line between where you are and where you want to be—happy.*

Therapy is anything but a straight line. Rather, it's a twisted road. Along its unpredictable path, therapists often lose sight of the essential teachings they wish to impart. They get lost in the details of the issues you're attempting to deal with and begin to believe that the details are what's most important. It's sad, but many therapists proudly proclaim, "You must take two steps backward in order to take one step forward." Most of the time this simply isn't true, and it's precisely the reason I have written this book. Not everyone wants or needs to take steps backward in order to move forward. In fact, my experience has been just the opposite. Many if not most people, given a choice, would love to start moving forward right now.

I suspect this is true for you, and I want you to have the choice. In this book you'll learn the best of what you could learn in therapy without what I call interference. I believe you'll see by the time you've finished reading that the interference of therapy, the tendency to go over and over the same issues, is actually part of the problem.

As with any other subject, there are a few essential ingredients that, once mastered, make everything that follows seem relatively easy. Once you learn the principle of addition, you can add up any two numbers. It doesn't matter whether they are $2 + 2$ or $6658 + 9981$.

To master anything, you need to understand the fundamental principles involved. Once you own the ideas, there's no need to keep discussing them, as is usually done in therapy. Once understood, the ten principles of growth-oriented, contented living can be used to bring back your emotional equilibrium regardless of the specific issue you confront. The principles are the most relevant information; once you understand them, happiness comes right away. There's no waiting period. You either know and trust the principles of happiness and see them working in your life, or you don't.

> *Show me a person who is waiting for life to be perfect before he allows himself to be happy and I'll show you a person who will never be happy.*

Whether your particular issue is a lack of money, your striving to be a better parent, the desire to improve a poor relationship, frustration at work or school, dealing with a difficult person, overcoming a troubled childhood, or ridding yourself of an addiction, the underlying solution is always the same—applying the principles of happiness to your problem to regain your psychological bearings. The dynamics of happiness are always the same. And as your emotional life improves, your newfound wisdom will guide you toward a better future.

> *Life is rarely the way we would like it to be. Life is as it is.*

As obvious as this seems, most people act as if the primary goal of life is to make it conform to some preconceived notions. To compound the problem, most of us attach our happiness to these preconceptions. We convince ourselves that we will be happy only when we earn more money, lose weight, or

get a different job. We put off our satisfaction and contentment until some later date.

The problem with this philosophy is that it is insatiable.
The same thinking that creates preconditions will continue to
do so once a condition is met. If you decide you must earn
more money before you allow yourself to feel happy, you'll invariably discover that still more money is necessary even if you
achieve your initial goal.

> *Don't set yourself up with one of the most popular
> prescriptions for unhappiness: Things must be differ-
> ent for me to be happy.*

A more practical way to look at the connection between
happiness and the achievement of goals is to view them as entirely separate entities. You can decide to put happiness first—
and you can also decide that, all things considered, you'd like
to earn more money. You'll begin to see that you've been living as if there were a necessary relationship between a certain
amount of money and happiness, when in fact no such relationship exists. You need to learn not to put the cart before
the horse.

Perhaps you're beginning to get sold on the idea that
learning the principles of happiness makes more sense than
struggling with your problems. But how can you be sure that
the principles you'll learn in this book are the most important
ones? Your common sense and the way you feel as you read
about these principles should convince you. You'll actually *feel*
the truth in what you're reading. You'll say to yourself something like "Of course that's true," or "If I were to implement
this principle, my life would improve." This is the way truth
works in your life.

The principles I discuss here have been taught by great
scholars, teachers, philosophers, and spiritual leaders for

thousands of years. They're simple and easy to understand, and all of them will hit home with your own wisdom and common sense.

At this point you may be asking yourself, "Can it really be this easy? Don't I need the experience of actually sitting down with a therapist and hashing it out?" The answer is: *It can be this easy*. In most cases, you really don't need a therapist. Consider this: An economist can spend her entire lifetime studying economics. She can spend many years writing a brilliant book about her discoveries. Then, in a few short hours, by reading her book, you can learn virtually everything she knows—after all, she has just taught you the basic principles of economics. You, the reader, get the benefit of her knowledge, but you didn't have to spend a lifetime studying the subject.

The same is true with personal growth. The principles you'll find are so simple and so natural that anyone can learn them, quickly and easily. Your educational history isn't a factor. Whatever your background, however damaging your childhood might have been, whatever problems you face, these principles still apply, and what's more, in most cases, they really are all you need to know.

One of the most important reasons this book can help you as much or more than therapy has to do with a problem I call analysis paralysis. This is what happens when you take a particular issue and analyze it to the point of reducing its value. Unfortunately, many therapists are masters of this art. Very often, a therapist has some helpful information to share, but the hours, and in some cases years, of analysis and detailed explanation dilute the effectiveness of the essential lesson.

For whatever reasons, society has come to accept the notion that happiness is elusive and complicated. Therapists have certainly done their part to reinforce this message. But it isn't true. What is true is this: *All legitimate principles of happier living are simple and easy to apply.*

* * *

As you read through the following principles I think you'll agree. Each principle is simple but powerful. If you make a gentle effort to put the principles into practice you will share the same positive feelings that other happy people enjoy! Good luck.

PART I

The Foundation and Theory of Shortcut Through Therapy

We are what we repeatedly do. Excellence, then, is not an act, but a habit.

—ARISTOTLE

A colleague recently addressed a group of two hundred graduate students in the field of mental health, presumably a most sophisticated audience. At one point during the speech he stopped to ask, "Is there anyone here who can give me a definition of 'mental health' and 'well-being'?" Dead silence. None of these highly educated students specializing in mental health had a clue.

This stunning lack of knowledge on the part of this particular audience flows naturally out of the traditional approach to mental health. Most professional mental-health education teaches some version of a medical model, with the absence of mental illness being the sole criterion for mental health. Traditional definitions of mental illness appear in an encyclopedic book called *The Diagnostic and Statistical Manual of Mental Disorders (DSM),* sometimes referred to as the Bible of traditional therapy. The DSM sets out a wide array of symptoms representing hundreds of disorders. The job of the therapist is to develop specific diagnoses that fit those in the manual based on a continuing analysis of the client's perceived problems and sources of unhappiness. If you were to look at the manual, you'd see that it contains hundreds and hundreds of pages of clinical diagnoses of mental illness—and absolutely no definition of mental health.

If you don't have something wrong with you, if you don't act or feel sick, you're assumed to be mentally healthy. This means that even though most mental-health practitioners— such as psychiatrists, psychologists, counselors, and stress consultants—are quite bright and articulate, they aren't necessarily trained in mental *health* at all. Instead, their training focuses exclusively on identifying, classifying, and treating mental *illness*.

I believe strongly that this single-minded focus contributes to the relatively limited effectiveness of traditional therapy. Instead of defining mental health as the absence of illness, I think of it in terms of the presence of more positive characteristics. The mentally healthy person is seldom irritated or annoyed, gets over adversity quickly, and exudes compassion for both himself or herself and others. That person is probably also highly creative, enjoys inner peace and contentment, and can deal effectively with the stress of day-to-day life.

But we're jumping ahead. Let's talk first about what really goes on when you begin therapy.

The Old-fashioned Way: Traditional Therapy

Many people think they need to be in traditional therapy if they're going to achieve happiness. When I speak of traditional therapy, I refer to any process, whether individual or group, that is based on the assumption that analyzing and discussing your problems will enhance your mental health. This definition includes a variety of types of therapy, including psychoanalytic, Jungian, and Gestalt.

One of the first things you need to understand about traditional therapy is that it almost always emphasizes identifying and treating problems. When you first sit down with your therapist, the conversation is usually about overcoming some identified difficulty. Regardless of the particular treatment approach, therapeutic goals are seldom phrased in terms of reaching a more positive state of mental health.

What Do All Traditional Therapies Have in Common?

Most people (my ongoing informal survey says 85 percent) who enter therapy are seeking to improve their life permanently. They want to develop independence, the ability to thrive on their own. They don't want to become dependent on the therapist. However, most approaches to therapy encourage just such dependence.

As far as I'm aware (and bear in mind that I'm not a clinical psychologist), virtually all existing approaches to therapy focus directly on the illness, unhappiness, or immediate concerns of the client. Therapists traditionally address specific problems, explore the thoughts and feelings associated with them, and delve into the client's childhood and situation in life. Traditional therapies assume that our problems are deeply rooted and extremely complex, and that the only way to deal with them is with intense analysis by an expert. None of them are fully committed to general, wellness-oriented solutions that help the client conquer unhappiness by building on his or her own inner strength. I don't know how many times I've had new clients at my stress center who say something like, "After three years of weekly therapy at one hundred dollars per hour, my therapist has a new swimming pool and I have the satisfaction of knowing that I can articulate my problems better than I could when I started. But I feel stressed out and I'm still frustrated."

Focusing on a specific worry in a therapy session may allow

the client to feel as if he or she is being listened to, and in many instances may even lead to a solution for that particular worry. But the client simply comes back for the following session with yet another worry. Given the emphasis on identifying issues (or problems) in therapy, the client doesn't learn to do anything else. At the same time, because the therapist seems concerned and empathic, the client may feel justified in the belief that his or her worries are legitimate. Respecting the therapist—who is, after all, a trusted authority figure—may just lead the client to keep on dealing with all those individual little problems.

There's been a great deal of interest in recent years in the so-called inner child. There is an entire movement devoted to tracing the effects of our early-childhood environments on our adult lives, with a general orientation toward blaming almost any dysfunction on "inner child" issues. Many therapists make this the focus of therapy, exploring the painful aspects of childhood—lack of attention, abandonment. For one hour, each and every week, the client's attention is riveted to the most painful aspects of his or her childhood.

While many clients certainly have had painful experiences in childhood, I argue that they're not really that important. What's important is not getting so caught up in the details of what happened decades ago that it hinders the development of positive mental health. As long as the therapy is dealing with many smaller issues, you'll be stuck in one place; you'll be unhappy. Many therapists see any expression of anger by the client as evidence of damage during childhood. This interpretation leads the therapist to conclude that the client needs *more* therapy, more work on the "inner child" to uncover additional trauma, and more excavation of pain and suffering. Does that sound healthy to you?

It's important to recognize that therapists are not trying to keep you unhappy. It's just that they've been trained to look for pathology instead of healthy states of mind. I recently read a case study of a client who'd had almost two hundred sessions with a therapist. Despite his large emotional and financial investment, it didn't seem that he was any happier or more contented than when he started. Virtually every session had been spent in talking about what was bothering him or how he felt about the fact that he was bothered, or in little arguments with the therapist about how to interpret his reactions. Nevertheless, the therapist was quite pleased that his client had developed a way of "trying to understand himself more fully." Do you think another two hundred sessions would make the situation any better?

While there are no firm statistics on the number of hours the average client spends with a therapist, individuals who come to my stress management center consistently tell me that they've spent somewhere between two and five years in therapy. Almost always, they've had one or more hourly sessions per week throughout this period. Even making a low estimate, this means that the average person in therapy spends more than a hundred hours discussing, analyzing, and speculating about his or her problems and unhappiness.

In short, the question asked most directly in traditional therapy is: "What's wrong?" I challenge you to ask yourself: "What's right? And how can I build on my strengths and become more mentally healthy?"

The Effects of Insecurity

During the past decade I've taught many clients and friends to deal with stress and to appreciate the art of happiness. One of the most important things I've learned is that when a person is already feeling threatened or insecure, the last thing you want to do is ask him or her to focus on the problem. The result nearly 100 percent of the time is that the individual is propelled into even greater insecurity and a lower emotional state.

Whether the client realizes it or not, the therapist's constant probing questions are experienced as attacks, and the natural reaction is to set up defenses. The client may retreat internally, offering whatever answer he or she believes the therapist wants to hear so that the therapist will stop probing into those painful areas.

A client who recently took the licensing exam to become a therapist told me about a question on the exam. It read: "What does it mean when a client begins to appear happy in a session?" The obvious response to this question, probably consistent with your first reaction, is that this reflects an improvement in the client's state of mind. He or she simply feels better. But according to this licensing exam, the correct answer is that the client is probably denying that he or she has problems or trying to avoid dealing with an important issue. If your therapist doesn't believe you when you tell him or her you're happy, how can you make progress? Even if you win, in the sense of being happier, you lose because your therapist doesn't believe you.

Let's reflect on what happens in traditional therapy, and discuss some alternative approaches. Had a woman come to my stress management center as a client and told me about the problems and negative events of the previous week, I might have shifted the discussion to moods in general, explaining that it was natural for her to feel different depending on her current state of mind. I'd help her learn to recognize her inner mood (or state of mind) and to avoid panicking when she was not at her best. Instead of encouraging her to recount her feelings of the previous week, or asking her how she was feeling at the moment, I would have put the focus on teaching her to achieve—and maintain—a deeper state of mental health. By reaching this state, she would learn many things:

- Not to be so totally concerned with the way she was feeling.
- To gain insight from her past, but without being adversely affected by it.
- To accept her current feelings, whatever they might be, without being frightened by or concerned about them.

- To see her feelings as an internal monitor to let her know when she was on track and when she needed to make mental adjustments.
- To use her feelings, even the ones she didn't like, to her own advantage.

As a result of all these learning experiences, she would leave my office on an emotional high, knowing that last week's feelings don't have to affect the way she feels today. She would come to the conclusion that recounting her feelings of last week—or her feelings of ten years ago—won't help her improve the quality of her life today.

Many of us grew up with too little love, too little positive attention, too many demands on us, poor role models. But you can't go through life using those misfortunes as excuses to avoid personal responsibility for who you are and what you can become. It seems to me that the underlying solution is fairly straightforward: We need better training to help us return to the basics, a crash course on how we're wired as human beings. We need to understand what makes us tick and what makes us fall apart, and relearn the art of living a happier and more secure life.

Recently I've been working with Susan, a rape victim who had previously been in traditional therapy. She complained that even though she had learned how to express herself about the trauma and to accept the emotional fallout, she continued to suffer from extreme stress. Part of the earlier work had involved visualizing the rape and then making mental "shifts"—that is, re-experiencing or pretending it were different—in the way she experienced it. Again, the focus of therapy was on the painful event itself rather than getting beyond it. No wonder she continued to feel stressed out!

Our work together was much simpler and far less painful. Rather than getting Susan to acknowledge and relive painful thoughts and memories, we spent our time figuring out how she could teach herself not to be so negatively affected when painful thoughts entered her mind; in other words, building up a foundation of wellness (i.e., learning to be happier, independent of her past *or* current circumstances) to insulate her from the impact of negative feelings when painful thoughts and memories surfaced. In a surprisingly short period she learned many important things:

- That she would probably always have painful thoughts to contend with—and that she could live with those thoughts, even using them in a positive way.
- *Not* to push her thoughts away, or pretend they aren't there; instead, she learned to accept them for what they are—her own thoughts.
- To be less frightened by her own thoughts, whether they were about the rape or about other aspects of her life.
- That attributing a great deal of significance to her thoughts and memories was one reason she continued to feel stress. She learned to give her thoughts less significance and to dismiss them more quickly, thus bringing herself back to the present whenever she experienced negative emotions.
- That her painful thoughts tended to crop up whenever she felt insecure. From this lesson she learned to recognize the times when she felt insecure, so as not to revert automatically to painful thoughts.

When you're considering treatment alternatives and trying to decide what to do about your problems or unhappiness, it's important to ask yourself, "Where do I want to go from here?" and "Is the process I'm going through (or about to go through, or considering going through) really going to bring me there?" Give honest answers to those questions before you make important decisions—they will determine the path you eventually take.

Getting Caught Up in Your Thinking

The trick in learning to be more contented in your life is to remain as much as possible in the present. A good mental exercise would be to try to catch yourself in the act whenever you find yourself mentally reviewing your past. After you come to understand the clear difference between learning from your past and becoming immersed in it, you'll be free to learn from your experience and grow in all ways.

When I speak in public, I often base my entire speech on the seemingly simple idea that getting caught up in a particular problem or issue is likely to cause more harm than good. The idea I try to get across is this: The fact that you're caught up in your thinking contributes more to your stress than the specific details of whatever it is you're caught up in.

This does not mean that what you're concerned about isn't important. It probably is, and you may need to do something about it eventually. But given the importance of your thoughts in determining the way you feel, the more caught up you get in anything in particular, the worse you'll feel in general.

When you feel low as a result of getting all caught up in a particular problem, you just aren't at your best. Among other things, you lose your ability to learn and to reflect, and you can't learn from your therapist—even if what the therapist has to teach you is truly relevant or important.

But if you look carefully at most forms of traditional therapy, you'll discover something very interesting. In almost all cases, the therapist *encourages* the client to get caught up. While few therapists would come right out and say they do that, actions speak louder than words. Here's what I mean:

THERAPIST: How are you feeling right now?

CLIENT: Not that great, actually. Kind of depressed.

THERAPIST: I know it's going to be difficult for you, but I thought we could focus, at this point, on the ways that your parents didn't allow you to be all you could be. You see, part of your problem today has to do with the way you related to your parents' suggestions that you weren't enough—and the way you internalized those suggestions. In order to resolve your inner conflicts, we need to look at the cause of your feelings.

CLIENT: That sounds like an okay idea. But I don't know exactly where to start. There were so many times when I was young that my parents, my mother in particular, made me feel unloved. It makes me sad to think about it.

THERAPIST: It's certainly okay that you're sad—let's go with your feelings rather than push them away. Let's begin with your mother. Can you give me an example of a time when you feel that your mother was cruel to you? I know there were many instances—but try to share one that you think epitomizes the way your mother made you feel.

CLIENT: Well, this one time—God it was horrible.

THERAPIST: It's okay. Don't push it away. Please continue.

CLIENT: I was with a group of six or seven of my friends, at home. I must have been twelve or thirteen. We were talking about guys. You know, teen stuff. I must have forgotten—no I did forget to do my chores and my mom went ballistic on me. She stormed into my room with my friends there and made a scene. She went on and on for what seemed like forever about what a stupid, spoiled bitch I was. It was horrible. I mean I haven't even thought about it for a long time. It was really bad.

THERAPIST: It sounds horrible and painful. How did it make you feel?

CLIENT: Small. Ashamed. Like a nothing.

THERAPIST: Go on. What else?

CLIENT: My mom made my friends go home. I was really embarrassed.

THERAPIST: And you get embarassed easily today, don't you.

CLIENT: I don't know. I just feel terrible. I mean, my mom probably did the best that she could. It just didn't seem very good.

THERAPIST: Don't feel like you have to give excuses for your mom. Let's go back to the way you felt when she belittled you as she did.

CLIENT: I don't know what else to say. It was awful. It was painful.

THERAPIST: Our goal is to get you to be as truthful as possible about the way you feel now and the way you felt as a child. I think you're doing really well and I'm proud of your progress. We're just about out of time—but this week I want you to think about other times that your mother made you feel small and weak. Don't push your feelings away. Deal with them the best you can, and next week we'll work with those feelings. Are you okay?

CLIENT: I don't know. I guess so. See you next week.

I ran this example by a dozen therapists. The overwhelming consensus was that this was a fair example of a typical segment of a typical session. In fact, the majority felt that this fictitious therapist was insightful and compassionate.

So what's the problem?

Look back at the first question the therapist asked the client and notice the response. The client is already sad, not feeling well, feeling insecure.

There is an important principle to be aware of in this example. When people are upset, when they lose their bearings, when they are down, depressed, insecure, angry, and so forth, their capacity to be reflective and introspective is greatly reduced (if not lost); it becomes extremely difficult to learn, have insights, gain perspective, and grow. This is true for all of us.

We'll come back to this specific example in a moment. But before we go on consider the following two very important points:

1. *You feel the way you do because of the thoughts you are thinking.* In other words, the feelings you have don't exist on their own. It's impossible to feel sad without having sad thoughts, angry without having angry thoughts, and so forth. If you need to verify this idea for yourself, you can try a simple experiment. What would you absolutely have to do if your goal was to get yourself angry? Without exception, you'd have to *think* of something that made you angry in order to feel angry. The same is true with all emotions. The chain of events is always the same: You think and then you feel.

2. *The fact that you're caught up in your thinking is ultimately more relevant to the way you feel than whatever you're thinking about.* Again, it's not the specific details that you're concerned with, but the fact that you're entertaining those concerns to begin with that counts most.

The client, in this instance, was already sad when she entered her therapist's office. This exchange, like so many supposedly therapeutic exchanges, was designed to assist the client to grow. But what really happened?

The client was innocently encouraged to get even more caught up in her thinking. I say innocently because it's very doubtful that the therapist had this goal in mind—the therapist was just doing what he or she felt was in the client's best interest. Nevertheless, in an already low state of mind, the client was directed to think of and focus on specific details (thoughts) that were painful. If it's true that we feel the way we do because of the thoughts we think, then the end result of this type of exchange is always that the client feels even more negative and insecure. In this more negative state of mind, learning is extremely difficult.

The client in this example is now involved in a potentially never-ending cycle. The more she thinks about her mother and the painful aspects of her childhood, the more depressed and upset she is going to feel. Her therapist may decide to ask probing questions for the next three sessions—or the next three dozen. Whatever the therapist chooses to do, one thing is certain: The client is going to get even more caught up in the details of what happened because the emphasis isn't on the fact that she's caught up but on the specific details and analysis of the conflicts she is caught up in.

The truth is, when you are "caught up" in anything, you lose your wisdom and common sense—it could be your childhood, your future, your finances, your sex life, a relationship, your work—whatever. The sad aspect of this "trap" is that even if you are lucky—even if you have an excellent, caring therapist who eventually helps you have an insight, you are probably going to be "bummed out" when you have the insight.

For instance, in our example above, let's assume that three weeks later the client does have the realization that her tendency to feel embarassed in public is linked to her mother's treatment of her when she was a child. This insight would have come after weeks of torment, bad feelings, probing, analysis, and sadness—which usually results in a person's feeling defeated by his or her own insight. The way that would typically play itself out would be for the client to say or think something like "My mom was really difficult and I can see why I've had such a tendency to feel embarassed for so long."

It's important to understand that when people feel defeated or depressed by their own insights, the likelihood of their behavior actually changing is close to nonexistent. In other words, the insight simply amounts to additional information to the client—a peripheral insight rather than an internal shift. The client has learned nothing in this example to prevent her from getting just as upset the next time she thinks about her childhood. Proof of this lies in the millions upon millions of clients who regularly seek the help of therapists.

Years after learning the damage inflicted upon them by their parents, clients are still just as immobilized, upset, and neurotic as they were the day they learned about "why" they are so unhappy.

Keep in mind, too, that when you're not "caught up" about something—those moments, minutes, days, weeks—when you're *not* focused on a problem, you don't feel the effects of those thoughts, real or imagined. When you're actively engaged in something else—work, play, spending time with your children, making love—the problem disappears. With this in mind, the client in our example isn't a victim of her mother—she's a victim of being caught up in her thoughts about how bad her childhood was. This is a critical distinction. I'm not suggesting that the client didn't have a difficult childhood. She did. I'm also not suggesting that her mother (and father) didn't affect her in some negative ways. They did. What I'm suggesting is that the negative events of your life only need to affect you while they're happening.

The difference between many "traditional" therapies and the approach toward happiness you are about to experience is that many approaches are designed to get you even more caught up in what's wrong with your life than you already are. My goal, in contrast, is to teach you to avoid getting caught up altogether. And when you learn to avoid getting caught up, two things will happen. First, your experience of life will begin to change. You will feel happier, more satisfied, and more joyful. Second, as you avoid getting too caught up in your thinking, you will begin to access your own wisdom on a far more regular basis. In this way, you will begin to see answers to the questions and problems that you used to be so conflicted about!

When you learn to avoid being caught up, whether it's with your therapist, with friends or a spouse, or even with your own thoughts, you are able to maintain and access your own healing wisdom. You are able to keep your emotional bearings, be reflective, and maintain perspective. When you aren't caught up, you can learn from your past, your mistakes, and your personal successes. You can begin catching yourself in the act as you are thinking in negative, self-defeating ways. You can learn to say to yourself, "Whoops, there I go again. I'm getting too analytical about this. I'm getting too caught up." As you learn this skill and as you practice it, you will find that you can step back from your problems as a way to actually solve them. If something is right in your face it's often difficult to see whereas when you take a step back, it becomes very clear.

Catching yourself in the act of dysfunctional thinking is a very powerful tool. It allows you to maintain a better feeling within yourself. The goal, you will see, is to "catch yourself" early in the process, before your thinking gets out of hand.

Each of the principles laid out in *Shortcut Through Therapy* has, as one of its main objectives, to help you avoid being caught up in your thinking. Each will assist you in maintaining a broad perspective so that you can learn from your childhood, you can learn from your mistakes, and most important, you can learn to enjoy your life, even though it hasn't been perfect. The principles will allow you to have many of the insights you might experience in therapy, but instead of being depressed by the insights you achieve, you will feel inspired by them.

There's a really important distinction here between my view of therapy and more traditional, analytical therapies. The traditional process usually encourages clients to pay attention to *specific* thoughts and inner mental experience in great detail. And not just any thoughts, either—the focus is almost always on the negative. This orientation flows naturally out of the medical model of therapy, as I discussed earlier, which leads both the client and the therapist to actively search out the underlying "illness."

It's true that being honest about how you feel is essential for you to get better. But if you don't learn *how* to feel better—in a positive sense—the therapy process can be a bit like a cat chasing its tail. Even if the therapy teaches you to be open and honest about your negative feelings, this alone won't make you feel better. Ideally, you should reach a point where you can tell your therapist: "All week I felt terrific and grateful to be alive!" However, most traditional therapists don't push you in this direction. Instead, if you tell such a therapist how good you feel, he or she might well respond with a question like "Was there anything that happened last week that was particularly difficult?" And as soon as you respond by dredging something up, you're caught up again. Right back in the loop!

The Key to Personal Growth: Your Mind

Your mind serves you in two important ways. First, it's a storage vault for information and experiences, the computer that analyzes, compares, relates facts, and draws conclusions. Second, your mind is a channel for the transmission of wisdom and common sense. This part of the mind deals with what might be called matters of the heart. It's this part of your mind that is the source of your contentment, joy, common sense, personal growth, and wisdom.

If you think about it, you can see how inappropriate it would be to use a computer to solve difficulties in a marriage or another heart-related problem, or to decide how to talk to your five-year-old daughter about discipline or to your teenager about drugs. This type of interpersonal issue requires gentleness, insight, and real wisdom. Yet using your computer is *exactly* what you do when you sit down with a therapist to analyze your problems. Unless you learn to understand and value the part of your mind that deals with matters of the heart, you'll have no alternative but to call on the computer part when you deal with personal issues. In all likelihood, you'll find that the solutions you arrive at are unsatisfactory and not all that positive.

Consider the examples of Ruth and Beth, each of whom recently experienced a traumatic breakup with her romantic partner. Ruth would fall into my category of mentally healthy. She certainly felt pain, but she knew she could bounce back. She never considered doing anything extreme; her mental health wouldn't allow her to. Her self-esteem and wisdom reminded her that despite the temporary emotional setback, everything would eventually work out.

Beth, however, had extremely low self-esteem and very poor mental health, according to my definition. What would she do? It's impossible to predict for sure, but we do know that if a person's self-esteem is low enough, he or she is more likely to take irrational, self-defeating actions when bad things happen.

A person who has a positive sense of self-esteem and inner peace is better able to handle adversity effectively—to take positive actions rather than harming himself or herself and even ruining his or her life. While no one wants bad or painful things to happen, stressful things do happen to all of us. Those of us who can develop and maintain a state of genuine mental health will deal with those events better, and have a smoother life as a result.

For that matter, developing positive self-esteem and mental health makes things a lot easier even when you're not having problems. A person with high self-esteem and inner peace knows how to truly enjoy life during more peaceful periods, while a person who lacks positive mental health just feels relieved by a temporary break from problems. Instead of shifting his or her state of mind toward gratitude, a person with lower self-esteem remains pessimistic and may spend the supposedly peaceful period bracing for that next crisis.

What Is Mental Health?

Here's a useful way to think about mental health:

Mental Health/Happiness

contentment, joy, humor, wisdom, common sense, personal insight, seeing opportunities and solutions, gratitude, kindness, service toward others

---

Mental Illness/Unhappiness

depression, reactivity, feeling sorry for oneself, seeing only problems, judgment, feeling criticized, irritation, annoyance, defensiveness, anger, jealousy

Everything above the line represents what we should strive for—a positive state of mental health that allows us to be happy and yet respond to life's real concerns. Everything below the line represents the things we really don't want to be—unhappy, with lots of negative attitudes that ultimately prevent us from responding to life's challenges.

In other words, even though the difficulties we experience vary considerably in duration and severity, there's one important constant: how we relate to what happens. The same event that one person sees as a simple challenge may be experienced by someone else as overwhelming. The first person will deal with the challenge creatively; the other person may end up having a nervous breakdown.

Please understand that this doesn't mean you're not going to be hurt, or that you won't mourn when traumatic events happen. You will. The message is that the dynamics of mental health and the dynamics of stress are always the same, two sides of the same coin. So while you can't always avoid being sad or angry—perhaps you shouldn't even try to avoid it—you can learn to avoid turning something that makes you sad into something that ruins your life or immobilizes you. You can learn to take even the most difficult experiences in stride. Even when really terrible things happen, your inner strength will empower you to feel free to move beyond it. You'll know that you have the strength and the tools to gravitate back toward your true state of mental health when the time is right.

Mental health means:

- That you have your own inner intelligence, a source of wisdom, that is stronger than any problem you might face.
- That you have tremendous power over your own mind.
- That you can and should take charge of your own thoughts and realize that they have no power to hurt you without your own consent.

> *When you operate from a truly healthy state of mind, you can recognize your destructive patterns for what they are and make changes as needed. You learn to live the happy life you've always wanted.*

We all have our share of what I call emotional fits. In fact, it's emotional fits that keep most therapists in business. My experience, however, has been that it's far more useful to build up your own self-understanding and self-esteem. Doing so will help you in *all* situations. Your own life-changing insights can prevent most emotional fits from occurring in the first place. One result: There's less need for the therapist to diagnose, analyze, and discuss each specific emotional problem or feeling as it arises.

One of the most important things I've learned is that everyone has the ability to attain his or her own state of self-knowledge. I've often worked with clients who, after learning to achieve a higher degree of contentment, become extremely reflective about their childhoods, including the negative aspects. However, they don't turn to childhood because I have been probing; they do so because their own inner wisdom has guided them in that direction.

I strongly believe that the key to living a truly happy life is to create new solutions to old problems by shifting the way you look at life. These shifts are achieved by understanding basic principles of life rather than just sorting through endless details. You can think of this process of creating healthier perspectives as climbing a series of rungs on a ladder, with each rung contributing to a more deeply positive feeling about life.

Your level of well-being and mental health at any particular moment is shaped by the way you perceive your life. Think of a simple scale—what I call the Ladder of Well-Being—that ranges from 1 to 10:

10 Contentment/Mental Health/Happiness
9
8
7
6
5 Indifference/Mediocrity
4
3
2
1 Unhappiness/Mental Illness

Most of us fall somewhere in the middle most of the time. If your state of mind is generally around 4 or 5, the way you think about all aspects of your life will be very different than if you were up around 7 or 8.

If you're in a really low mood, at the bottom of the scale, you'll feel sorry for yourself and probably be angry at others and the world in general. If someone asks you to discuss your past when you're down there, what will you say? If you're like most people, you'll describe a past filled with hardship and difficulty, and talk about how unhappy you are with your life. However, if you were asked the identical question while in an extremely positive state of mind, it's very likely your answer would be quite different.

I use this exercise regularly in working with stressed-out clients, and virtually all of them are shocked when they realize just how different life looks depending on how they're feeling. When they feel good, they look back at their childhoods with an entirely different perspective—regardless of the specific details. One client, for example, had a most unhappy childhood filled with real pain. When he first came in, he was down around 1 on the scale, and his typical comment about his past was something like "I hated my parents and still do. My life is just terrible." Before too long, however, he had moved several rungs up the Ladder of Well-Being. Then, when I'd ask him about his childhood, he'd make a comment to this effect: "Well, my parents did what they knew how to do. It wasn't very good, but it was what it was." He was the same person—he was just at a fundamentally different level of mental health and well-being.

A deeper and more broadly based appreciation of life can be developed in many ways, including some that might be very surprising. A client named Rachel provides an excellent example of how not getting caught up in details can help a person grow in a positive direction, even under the worst of circumstances. Rachel lost a close friend, but rather than grieving and suffering terribly, she learned from the experience. She came to a fundamental understanding of the meaning of gratitude after her friend died. She found peace, and in effect moved up one rung on the Ladder of Well-Being. She focused on the gratitude she felt for having known her friend and having had her in her life, rather than dwelling on her specific feelings of loss and sadness. She refused to get caught up in details that would have kept her from climbing the ladder. This experience helped her place a high priority on living each day as if it were her last.

What if Rachel had gone to a traditional therapist to help

her deal with her grief? First the therapist would have asked Rachel what was bothering her, leading immediately to a focus on the details of her friend's death. In fact, most therapists would expect Rachel to be pretty much immobilized by the experience she'd been through; and if Rachel didn't act that way, they would probably interpret it as meaning she was in denial about the incident and her underlying feelings. I would argue that this strategy would have prevented Rachel from learning the meaning of gratitude, and that she would never have stepped up that rung on the ladder. Rachel had lost almost all her sense of gratitude. Our sessions focused on how to re-integrate the feeling of gratitude (see chapter 8) into her life. She learned that her focus on the death pulled her away from her feeling of gratitude, while a focus on gratitude lifted her spirits and gave her greater perspective.

It's important not to misunderstand what I'm saying here. Obviously, Rachel might have benefited from a certain amount of focus, and it's also true that everyone has to grieve after a loss. What I am saying is that an excessive focus on the negative represents an obstacle to life-enhancing insights.

This does not mean that you should *never* reflect on both the positive and negative aspects of your own past. It's okay to do that, and in some cases probably important. But the key is to avoid getting lost in the content of your thinking and always to remain aware that you are in charge of your thoughts. You don't have to get caught up in irrelevant details. Instead, you can learn to consider those issues in a reflective way. In the process you'll become mentally healthy and keep yourself above the mental health baseline.

The Solution

As I've been explaining, most problems and unhappiness originate when you get stuck on something. If you're focused on little details, you have no way to see the more important solutions. Those solutions can only come into view when you learn

to see things in a fresh way, allowing your wisdom and common sense to take over. As you clear your mind of secondary
concerns, you'll use lessons from your own past to fuel your
personal growth. As your well-being and mental health move
in a positive direction, answers will come to you in ways you
never dreamed possible.

For example, you might have an insight: "I never realized
how defensive I can get with my husband when he offers a
suggestion," or "Gosh, I'm treating my kids exactly the way my
parents treated me." If you're in a negative or caught-up state
of mind when these thoughts occur, you'll probably just brush
them off or file them away in your memory bank. But if you're
in a truly positive and growth-oriented state of mind—if
you're receptive and ready to grow—these insights can create
an uplifting realization that can permanently alter your view
of reality.

Remember that the most profound answers in your life
may be the simplest. I recently had a client tell me, after the
briefest of conversations, "I think all my wife really wants from
me is for me to listen to her." Although he had previously
been in therapy for two years, he'd never come to this seemingly simple realization that he'd been searching so hard for.

This client's insight is particularly useful as an illustration
that increasing your sense of well-being is the ultimate vehicle
that fuels your insights—not rehashing your problems. We
weren't even discussing his marriage. We were talking about
the importance of gratitude. He was reflective, in a quiet and
peaceful state of mind, as he told me some of the things he
was most grateful for. Being listened to was on top of his list,
as it would be for many of us. Then, seemingly out of nowhere, he said, "Gee, I just realized I never really listen to my
wife." He went on to give me examples of times when he
thought he'd been listening to her—but really wasn't. Later I
received a wonderful call from his wife, asking me, "How did
you teach my husband to listen?" All I could say was "He
taught himself." When you teach yourself, through your own
wisdom and through moving up the rungs of the Ladder of

Well-Being, your insights will be rich, meaningful, and in all probability permanent.

I've discovered that human beings have an incredible resilience—we can bounce back from just about anything. Each of us has a self-correcting emotional system, and anyone can learn to make use of his or her own inner strength, even under the most stressful circumstances. As long as you avoid getting caught up in details—or focusing on aspects of yourself that are labeled dysfunctional—you too can begin to move up the rungs of the Ladder of Well-Being.

The remaining chapters will teach you about the ten principles that directly affect your ability to get in touch with your inner wisdom. After each chapter, it may be valuable to sit down and reflect on what you've read. Avoid analyzing yourself with questions like "To what extent do I already do what I have just finished reading?" Instead, receive each principle with a beginner's mind. Start fresh with each principle, absorb the basic idea, and you may find that your gentle attempts to put the principle to work in your life will bear remarkable fruit.

Some of the principles will be easier to digest than others. Don't worry about this; each principle operates independently of the others. Take them to heart one at a time, using each one to open a more serene part of yourself. You'll feel more peaceful; some of the old obstacles may fall away, and new insights will come into your mind. As you read the book you may find yourself experiencing a quieter state of mind. If so, enjoy it! When you're in a receptive and relaxed state of mind, the answers you need—the answers that reside within you— are most accessible. You'll discover that your own mental health is like a cork—it may be temporarily held down at the bottom of the ocean, but it always bobs back to the surface. You'll learn to drop your overactive, analytical, and conditioned thinking and begin developing totally new attitudes and ways of thinking that foster growth and enjoyment. Your mind will regain its sense of equanimity and peace.

So let the fun begin!

PART II

The Principles of Shortcut Through Therapy

PRINCIPLE ONE:
Make Yourself Happy

Be happy. It's one way of being wise.

—COLETTE

Take Responsibility for Yourself

Perhaps the basic message of all therapy, and thus the first principle we'll study, is that you and you alone are responsible for your own happiness. No one—not your parents, your spouse, your children, your friends, your coworkers, or your therapist—can live your life for you, nor can they make you happy. There are certainly many paths you can take toward happiness and personal growth, but you must walk them for yourself. You're the one who must change.

While the notion of taking responsibility for your own life may seem obvious, how many of us really do? How often we say to ourselves, "Why can't people be more friendly?" or "It makes me so mad when she says that," or "I wish she would act differently," or "I wish he weren't so critical of me." These, and many other statements and thoughts like them, suggest that somehow, in some way, someone *other* than you is responsible for your happiness. This type of thinking brings personal growth to a grinding halt and makes contented living all but impossible.

The illogical notion that someone else can make you happy sounds something like this: "If the world and all the people in it would only change, then I'd be happy."

Psychologist Wayne Dyer pokes fun at this idea like this: "Round up all the people who are making your life miserable and bring them to me. I will treat them, and then you'll be happier."

I have been teaching the art of reduced-stress living for ten years. Virtually all the clients I've worked with began their sessions with similar attitudes: "I'm stressed because my husband works too hard," or "I'm unhappy because my wife isn't as attracted to me as she once was." Almost always, a person's precondition for happiness lies in the belief that *someone else* must change before the person will allow himself or herself to feel better.

There's good news and bad news in this common belief. The bad news is that no one is going to change his or her habits, attitudes, beliefs, or behavior so that you can be a less stressed person. What's more, even if others did change, it wouldn't satisfy you for more than a few minutes. As one habit or behavior altered, you'd be looking for another improvement, and then another. Like a rat running through an endless maze, you'd be hooked on the hope that just around the corner, life would get better.

If you believe (even a little bit) that the answer to your inner turmoil lies in someone else's hands, you are assuring yourself a life of frustration. You may as well call yourself a victim because that's exactly what you will be, totally dependent on other people and their actions for your emotional well-being.

The good news is that once you stop blaming other people for your plight and put 100 percent of the responsibility for your happiness on yourself, it's easy and rewarding to get on a path toward a growth-oriented, happier life. After all, personal growth is just that—*personal*. It's about you, your inner world, your reactions to life, your judgments and attitudes. Personal growth is not about your husband, your wife, your parents, your children, or anyone else. Personal growth is about *your* ability to take responsibility for *your* own life and *your* own happiness. It's about *your* ability to choose the way *you* will react and interact in *your* life.

This first step of personal growth is in many ways the most important. If you think about it logically, nothing that follows is really possible until you make an absolute commitment to taking responsibility for yourself. It's ironic but true: Most people enter therapy for "personal growth" reasons but are initially resistant to the idea that *they* must change.

Be Pro-active

The decision to take responsibility for your own happiness is now widely being labeled "pro-active." This means not only taking charge of your own destiny but also realizing that each one of us is totally responsible for our own life. It means *never* waiting for someone else to change so that you can feel better about yourself.

> *Becoming pro-active means arriving at the conclusion that circumstances don't merely make a person, they reveal a person.*

Difficult circumstances are merely opportunities to demonstrate to yourself how you're doing with your life. If you have "difficult circumstances" and you're a pro-active person, you'll make the best of it. You'll find a way to use those circumstances to help you become a more self-sufficient, growth-oriented person. If you're *not* a pro-active person, those identical circumstances will be viewed as being to blame for your misery.

To a non pro-active person, circumstances become excuses for unhappiness and limitation: "I can't exercise because I have bad knees," "I can't maintain close friendships because my wife won't let me," "I can't spend time with my friends because I have small children," "I don't feel good about myself because my parents are still verbally abusive." These excuses, and thousands of others like them, are cop-outs that keep people from taking charge of their own lives.

Pro-active individuals live by a take-charge motto: *"There is no reason good enough to keep me miserable.* No matter what's going on, I have at least some control. Somewhere along the line I have made decisions that have contributed to where I am today. Luckily, I have the ability to decide how I am going to respond." In his classic book *Man's Search for Meaning*, Victor Frankl demonstrated that even in the midst of conditions so awful that most of us can't even imagine them (Nazi concentration camps), human beings have a powerful free will.

It's possible to choose inner peace and emotional well-being even when life isn't what we would like it to be.

Emotionally responsible individuals use their circumstances, whatever they are, however bad they seem, to grow. People who don't take responsibility for their own happiness feel abused and victimized by their circumstances. Often they build their entire life and sense of self-worth around the behavior and approval of others. They spend their lives looking over their shoulders hoping to be noticed, appreciated, and loved. They invest a great deal of time and energy in comparing themselves to others and seeking approval.

We often act like victims in subtle ways. It might happen at the post office when we think to ourselves, "These clerks seem to be trying to move as slowly as possible." Or we'll feel victimized when we don't get something we were hoping for—a package doesn't arrive, praise isn't bestowed, or someone is late or doesn't show up. We think, "Why are they doing this to me?"

If a self-reliant, responsible person, on the other hand, feels unhappy, he knows that somehow he is processing his thoughts in a way that is making him unhappy. Even if he doesn't know what he's doing to hurt himself, he is introspective enough to know that it's him doing it. This doesn't always translate into immediate joy, but it does put him in a position where eventual happiness, and certainly growth, are at least possibilities.

Examine the roots of the word responsibility—it means the ability to respond, to choose your response, to choose how you will process the events and circumstances in your life. In short, responsibility means the buck stops with you. You're in charge, not just when everything seems to be going okay, but all the time. Once you own this idea, trust it, and incorporate it into your life, you'll become hopeful. You'll find that it's a lot easier to control your own thoughts, responses, and emotions than it is to wait for the world to conform to your wishes. Whenever I hear someone say, "I can't control my reactions to life," I respond by asking simply, "Who can?" I ask this not to be crass or insensitive but to help empower the person to understand and believe that no one else can do it for him or her.

Don't Create "As If" Traps

The opposite of taking responsibility for your own happiness, of being pro-active, is being reactive, reacting to rather than choosing how to respond to life. Overly reactive individuals can be explained by a model I like to call the "As If" Trap.

Human beings have an amazing capacity to create a

thought and then carry that thought through time as if it were true. In other words, we learn to see cause-and-effect relationships between events and feelings that, on closer examination, don't necessarily exist.

When you're caught up in the complexity of an issue, it's difficult to see that you're the one making it complex.

Here are a few "As If" Traps that reactive people can easily fall into.

You fail at a task that is important to you and subsequently act as if there is a necessary relationship between failing at something and feeling bad. Every reactive person acts as if this connection really exists. Because it's disappointing when we fail, a feeling that most people have, it *seems* logical and truthful to act and feel disappointed. But is it, necessarily? It depends.

A woman, for example, who is reactive reacts to the way she is feeling and justifies that feeling in her own mind. The chain of events goes something like this: She fails, she feels bad, then she reacts to the way she's feeling by sulking and thinking about how she failed. She compounds the problem by thinking about it further and talking about it to others. In short, she acts as if it's necessary and appropriate to feel the way she does. She never bothers to question this apparent cause-and-effect relationship because she's too busy reacting to how she's feeling.

Alice, a client, felt extremely stressed each time her boss questioned her judgment. She reacted to any perceived disapproval by feeling, and usually acting, defensive. She often spent much of her day thinking about what must be wrong with her as well as harboring negative feelings toward her boss.

Alice said her previous therapist had convinced her that

her problem was "a deep-seated issue stemming from the disapproval she experienced from her parents." Despite holding on to this information for quite a few years, Alice remained defensive and still tended to get depressed. She and her therapist had "explored the roots" of her frustration, but her habit nevertheless always seemed to prevail.

Alice considered herself a pro-active individual, and in many areas, she seemed to be one. However, she had set up many "as if" relationships in her head without ever questioning their validity. Initially, when I introduced the subject, she quickly dismissed the information as "too simplistic." However, after thinking about it further, she began to laugh, saying, "I'll bet my therapist would see this as too simplistic as well." She was probably right.

Alice quickly realized that her destructive pattern lay in her assumption that it was necessary and appropriate to feel bad when someone in a position of authority criticized her. She began to see that she extended this "as if" thinking to the rest of her life as well. Indeed, she tended to get defensive when anyone offered her any suggestion.

She came to the conclusion that her insistence on knowing the "root reason" behind her defensiveness had actually hurt her more than it had helped. She realized that whenever she felt criticized, she quickly began resenting and blaming her parents, something that she claimed her therapist had actually encouraged. In our time together, Alice realized that blaming others is a non-pro-active response. She learned that what she really needed to do was to catch herself in the act just when she began feeling defensive. She learned to recognize her feeling of defensiveness as an internal signal, one that let her know that she had fallen back into the habit of "as if" thinking.

By the end of her experience with me, Alice was chuckling at her improvement. At times she still began to feel defensive when her boss (or someone else) offered a suggestion, but she was beginning to catch herself and her "as if" thinking earlier. The result of this understanding for Alice was that rather than

making a relatively simple habit of "as if" thinking into a lifelong struggle (as it was beginning to be in her therapy), she
turned her habit into a game. And she was winning.

*A pro-active person knows that she has a choice. She takes respon-
sibility for the way she is feeling rather than blaming her feelings on
her failure.* She knows she can either learn from the experience and move on, or dwell endlessly on her failure. She
didn't want to fail the task any more than anyone else would
have. But she understands that she doesn't have to act as if it's
carved in stone that she must spend the week feeling bad because of it. She takes full responsibility for the way she is looking at and thinking about the situation.

> **The shortest distance between where you are and
> where you want to be is an intention.**

Here's another example of an "As If" Trap: You had dysfunctional parents and a difficult childhood and you act as if
your childhood has a lot to do with your ability to be happy today. Is this true? Again, it depends on your belief. Of course
your childhood affected you, but you can only use this excuse
for so long. Do you believe there is a cause-and-effect relationship between a difficult childhood and the necessity of feeling
bad today? If so, you're a reactive person. You're reacting to
what seem to be logical beliefs and feelings based on your
experience.

But what about those people who had difficult and painful
childhoods but don't feel bad today? I know they exist because
I've worked with many of them. Are they naive? Are they repress-
ing their true feelings? I think not. They have overcome their
negative, difficult pasts and have become pro-active individuals.
They realize that they are the ones processing the information
about their childhoods within their own minds. Their parents
aren't involved anymore. Today it's just them and their thoughts.
This being the case, they can choose to dwell on how bad things

were, or they can choose otherwise. Power, to a self-responsible person, lies within the person's own thinking. Childhood is over. Obviously, unfortunate events did happen in childhood, and that's too bad. But today, right now, the past is only a memory. It's time to make new choices and to move on.

Let me give you an example of an "as if" discovery that I had about myself many years ago. For a long time I rushed around trying to "get everything done." Collecting achievements was the most important goal in my life. In short, I was acting as if the purpose of life was to accomplish as much as possible in as little time as possible. Although I sacrificed my personal happiness to achieve my goals, I believed it was necessary. If you had asked me at that time what my greatest personal weakness was, I would have responded confidently, "Not enough time." In reality, I used every waking second as efficiently as possible. I was almost always working, rushing, struggling to accomplish something. However, I felt victimized by my own schedule. Since I never questioned my basic "as if" assumptions about life, I continued to rush and be frustrated.

Like my earlier example, Alice, I had been in therapy at an earlier time in my life. Also like Alice, I had come to believe that my problem was very complex. I believed that my rushing around and sense of hurry stemmed from my belief that I wasn't good enough without my accomplishments. Despite several years of analysis and discussion, I maintained my business as if nothing had changed. It wasn't until I saw my own "as if" thinking that I was able to slow down and relax.

When I finally realized that I was living my life as if it were one big emergency, I was able to make a change. I made a shift from being a reactive person (reacting to my feelings of urgency and my belief that my early childhood was responsible for my frustration) to being a basically pro-active person (realizing that I'm the one in charge of my life, my goals, and my schedule). I was able to change a lifelong habit.

I want to share with you an experience I had with a client a few years ago. This gentleman came to me with a sad, drawn, and disturbed face. He slouched as he walked. He wouldn't look me in the eye. He was too upset to speak—except to say, "You'd be upset too." It turned out that the event he claimed had upset him had taken place *seven years before.* Not seven minutes or seven days, but seven years. Here was his problem: Seven years before he came to see me, he was in his last AA (minor-league) baseball game. He was playing left field. It was the last inning of the game and the batter from the opposing team hit the ball toward him. If he caught the ball, the game would end and his team would win. If not, a base runner would score and his team would lose. It was an easy catch, well within his proven ability. His family and many of his friends were watching. His team was counting on him.

By now, you've probably guessed that he missed the ball. He dropped it, and he was humiliated. He was the goat. People laughed. He let his team down. He vowed that he would never forgive himself. To put it in the terms we're discussing, he acted as if his life were ruined, his dreams were shattered, and his actions were unforgivable. He had carried this thought through time as if it were still true.

The key to understanding why this man was so upset over so little is this: He was on the opposite end of the spectrum from being pro-active. He was completely reactive. He believed it was carved in stone that he should blame himself for the rest of his life, and he didn't question the validity of this belief. He thought he couldn't be happy because he was a failure.

As extreme as this client was in his mental self-ambush, sadly he was really not all that different from the rest of us in that he didn't question his basic assumptions, his "as if" beliefs about life. We all have dozens, if not hundreds, of beliefs about life that we assume are true when, in fact, there is no cut-and-dried evidence that they are. We act as if our beliefs represent reality. We believe in thoughts like "I'm upset because Mary received the promotion instead of me," or "I can't feel secure until my income increases." These types of thoughts are mental traps that keep us stuck in believing that we must continue feeling bad.

They are subtle ways that we remain reactive rather than empowered individuals.

One key to becoming a pro-active, take-charge person is to become slightly suspicious of any of the basic beliefs and assumptions that seem to get in your way. You don't necessarily have to change any of your beliefs, but you do need to begin to ask yourself questions such as "How do I know that's true?" "Haven't I just assumed I was right?" "Couldn't I be wrong?" "Isn't it possible that I might be able to be happy *before* I increase my income?" Questions like these open the door to realizing that *you* are in charge of the answers you give to these questions. You can learn to discredit your usual way of seeing life and focus instead on the broader possibilities. You are only a victim of life if you believe you are a victim, if you tell yourself you are a victim, if you act like a victim, and if you choose to be a victim.

A friend of mine once said, "The shortest distance between where you are and where you want to be is an intention." This is certainly true with regard to taking responsibility for your own happiness—you must have the intention to do so. As you make this step a priority, you will see this principle manifesting itself in your life.

Become Inner-Directed

> *Inner-directed people are happy because they know that their life is a series of choices, and that they are in charge of those choices.*

Taking personal responsibility means becoming an inner-directed person. To be inner-directed means to look inside yourself for your own answers, to trust your own intuition and wisdom over and above anyone else's opinion, and to follow your own instincts. If you're inner-directed, you never rely on another person to make you happy and never give someone else the power to control your emotions. A commitment to being inner-directed means listening to yourself and relying only on *you* to make you happy.

Inner-directed people understand that they have choices in how to interpret, how to think, how to respond, how to behave, and how to change something if it isn't working. Because inner-directed people take responsibility for their own happiness, they never feel like victims, people who feel their lives are determined by, or dependent on, other people.

The temptation to live an outer-directed life is prevalent in our culture. A client named Alan was so concerned with other people's opinion of him that he built an expensive home in plain view of a major freeway. He told me he wanted people to drive by and say, "Hey, that's Alan's home. Isn't it nice?" His intense need for approval from others overshadowed his intense stated dislike of noise and confusion. He was so locked into his belief that other people could make him happy that he took his hopeful philosophy to new heights.

The trick for Alan was to learn to feel good without relying on other people. He learned to find more positive feelings within himself, building his foundation of emotional health. He learned to focus more on the present, to take his low moods less seriously, and to avoid negative thought attacks, a few of the topics you'll read about later.

I have never met a happy or contented person who isn't inner-directed, and I never expect to. Outer-directedness is entirely inconsistent with happiness. After all, happiness comes from within a person, not from the behavior of others or from certain circumstances. The first step in becoming a genuinely happy person, then, is to make a lifetime commitment to becoming more inner-directed than you already are.

Approval, as nice as it can be, is not a prerequisite to being a happy person.

Each of us has experienced a great deal of disapproval in our lives. For many of us, a vast majority of this disapproval has come from the people we love the most—our family and friends. Unfortunately there is no way to please everyone all the time. In fact, it's difficult to please almost anyone very much of the time. Disapproval is as predictable as the sun coming up in the morning.

Inner-directed people know that disapproval is inevitable. They never seek it out, but they do know it will come their way, at least some of the time. Far more important to an inner-directed person is to feel good about himself or herself and the decisions he or she makes. Inner-directed people ask themselves many times a day, "How do *I* feel about this decision?" "Is this what *I* really want to be doing?"

Inner-directed people are very willing to listen to others. Because they don't feel defensive or threatened when someone disagrees with them or sees something differently, they feel free to listen and evaluate, easily and peacefully, without an inordinate amount of emotional distraction.

Inner-directed people have learned that they will never consistently get the approval they expect or want from others, so they have simply decided to stop being so concerned about it. Instead, they turn inward for their own approval.

Love Yourself First

> *Self-love stems from an inner sense of security—the quiet knowledge that you're a special human being with unique talents and gifts to offer.*

Inner-directed, self-confident people are *not* conceited or self-absorbed. In fact, they're just the opposite. They feel so good about themselves that they have plenty of love and respect left over for other people. Inner-directed people often act in consistently loving ways because they have so much love inside themselves to give back to the world.

Many people would love to be kinder and more giving to their fellow human beings, but this admirable goal is unattainable without true self-love and self-respect. If you don't feel strong self-love you will be easily threatened by others and will be so wrapped up in your own needs and wants that it will be difficult, if not impossible, to be truly loving to others.

Strive to understand how everything good and worthwhile in your life stems from this loving sense of inner direction: Your best decisions are made when you feel best about yourself; you're kinder to others when you feel inwardly secure, and you take life less seriously when you feel calm and relaxed. Unfortunately, many people reject the idea of self-love because they confuse it with narcissism, when in fact the two are not related.

In contrast to self-love, narcissism stems from insecurity, an outward-directed, "looking over my shoulder to see who is looking at me" attitude. On the surface, a cleverly disguised narcissist can appear to have too much self-love, but in reality, he or she has far too little. Narcissism will eventually show itself as selfishness, lack of compassion for those less fortunate, arguing with others, and frantic approval-seeking. People who enjoy genuine self-love, however, already feel good about themselves before they meet other people; they have no interest in proving themselves to others or in attempting to gain their approval.

The easiest way to increase your self-love is to recognize that you were born with it. Self-love and self-esteem are inherent in human beings, but are unfortunately covered up within a few years by insecure thoughts about ourselves that we learn to accept as truth. We think: "I'm no good," "No one likes me," and so forth. These and other thoughts like them, if left unchecked and unchanged, will eventually distort the way you see yourself.

Our parents and other significant role-models give us the

same message that was given to them: You're not good enough the way you are; you must be better.

A simple example of this process can be seen at practically any playground in America. Watch a small child practicing his balance. When he falls down, he picks himself up. He might even laugh at himself. Then one day, his parent or someone else says to him, "Hey, don't fall down," or "Johnny balances better than you do," or some other statement suggesting that falling down isn't okay—having better balance than you presently do is better.

A child quickly realizes that he gets more positive praise for balancing than he does for falling down. He hears moans and groans and comparisons when he falls and praise when he "succeeds." Soon, he begins to take to heart his own thoughts like, "You dummy, you're no good," and so forth.

You can see the innocence of this process. The parent is simply trying to motivate the child to improve, and the child is simply trying to please the parent. If the child didn't internalize negative thoughts, the entire process would be harmless. But, almost without exception, he does internalize his thoughts. He begins to believe the negative thoughts he is having about himself.

A good way to prevent the habit of internalizing negative thoughts is to teach kids to ignore them. In other words, teach them that they don't have to take their own negative thoughts seriously; they have the power to dismiss them. If they have a thought like "I'm not good enough" or "I'm not pretty enough," they can simply recognize and accept that everyone has negative thoughts from time to time—but happy people learn to ignore or dismiss them.

But you don't have to be a child to understand this simple truth. At any point in your life you can decide to ignore the negative thoughts you have about yourself. You can begin by understanding that thoughts are just that: thought. There is nothing holding them in place other than your decision that they are true and significant.

Once you learn to ignore negative thoughts you have about

yourself, you'll be on your way to a shining sense of self-worth. People who take responsibility for their own happiness do just that: They realize that they themselves create the thoughts that bring them negative feelings, and that they are also the only ones who can dismiss those thoughts (a skill you'll learn in chapter 3).

To create greater self-love, make a commitment to become more inner-directed in your life. Such a commitment sheds new light on exactly why you're here on this planet, and what you must do. As Joseph Campbell put it, you find and follow your own bliss.

A commitment to inner-directed living is the most satisfying, reassuring, and eye-opening endeavor you can undertake, an antidote to all the confusion and resentment you've ever felt in your life. Without such a commitment, you must wait for the world to conform to the way you would like it to be, which, of course, will never happen.

Make this commitment today and you'll be forever glad you did. Remember, the key to making the commitment is having the intention of doing so. Strive to be inner-directed. If you catch yourself blaming others, stop your inner thoughts that imply that anyone other than you is responsible for your happiness.

As you become more inner-directed, you'll see that the frustration, anger, resentment, criticism, and judgment you feel toward others has always come from inside you—not from the world you live in, and not from the people you live with. Anger, disapproval, and frustration stem from the way we think and from our expectations; they come from inside us, from the way we see the world. So too does love. When you say to someone, "I love you," that love is coming not from the person you're directing your love toward, but from feeling deep inside you.

One immediate and reassuring payback from understanding this notion is that it applies to everyone else as well. Whether it's your parents, your children, your coworkers, or your friends and neighbors, any disapproval aimed in your direction is coming from the person aiming it. You're not responsible for it, and it doesn't mean there is anything wrong with you.

> *Looking for and finding fault with others will do nothing in the long term to make your life better.*

This is not a prescription for avoiding responsibility, or for refusing to listen to suggestions from others. It is a blueprint for letting go of the needless heartache that so often accompanies disapproval from others. When you see clearly where disapproval comes from, it becomes far easier not to take it personally.

Be Honest with Yourself

Inner-directed people don't blame others for their unhappiness. Instead, they attempt to see whether or not they are contributing to the problem at hand, and if so, they attempt to mitigate their part. Outer-directed people do just the opposite. They always look for "who's to blame" or "who's at fault." Obviously if someone has truly wronged you, you may need to take corrective action, but inner-directed people are more concerned with working on themselves and freeing themselves to make themselves happier. Inner-directed people don't want others to be wrong; they know that making someone else wrong has absolutely nothing to do with making themselves happy.

Looking at your own contribution to a problem is not the same as actively seeking out your own faults or berating yourself. Instead, it often takes the form of a simple statement to yourself such as "Maybe I'll see this more clearly tomorrow." This is in sharp contrast to an outer-directed person, who would probably be thinking something like "I'd be happier if my partner were different."

> *Inner-directed people know that it's impossible to change other people—and even more importantly, they wouldn't be interested in doing so even if they could.*

Looking for someone else to blame won't improve *your* life. This statement holds true regarding your parents. Sure it's a fact that your parents helped to mold you into the person you are today—positively as well as negatively—but to focus on this fact and on what they may have done wrong is ultimately counterproductive. It may be a frequent technique of therapy, but it's only a convenient way to blame others. What will improve the quality of your life is a commitment to turning inward, a commitment to changing what you can about your own life.

> *Looking over your shoulder and comparing yourself to others is a prescription for pain and unhappiness.*

Inner-directed people aren't concerned with how they are doing relative to others. Although they may compete with others in their careers or in other environments, they don't equate their self-worth with their competitive performance. To be concerned with how you are doing relative to other people is completely inconsistent with inner guidance. There will always be people who are more talented than you are, work harder than you do, and seem to have had better luck than you've had. Likewise, there will always be people who are less talented than you are, put forth less effort than you do, and have been less fortunate than you've been. Remember, no two people are alike and no two people have identical circumstances. Even if they did, no two people would process their thoughts about those circumstances the same way.

Be Spontaneous and Flexible

Inner-directed people tend to be spontaneous. Regardless of the complexity of their circumstances, they have the capacity to change direction in midstride because they are committed not to consistency but to the truth.

One's inner truth is the sense of knowing what is right or wrong at any given moment. For example, your inner truth might be that it's appropriate, even critical, to spend time with a particular friend. You can't necessarily explain why you have this feeling. You just do—and you know it's right. However, this inner truth can change. Your feeling of need to be with this friend can go away—therefore your inner truth changes. If you are an inner-directed person you honor this change and accept it. You know that your sense of knowing— your inner truth—isn't stagnant. It changes.

Outer-directed people, however, put their faith and sense of well-being in external sources. For example, their friend may have said to them, "It's important that I see you." Then, if circumstances change and the friend says, "It's not as important as I thought—our meeting can wait," the externally oriented person feels immobilized. He has put the source of his own happiness in other people's hands. He feels angry or sad that his friend changed plans. He doesn't honor the fact that his friend's inner truth has changed—and he probably doesn't honor this in himself as well.

An inner-directed person, knowing that "truth" can change from moment to moment, can move into a new career even though he has always done something else. He can have a change of heart and decide to love someone even though he has been upset with her for a long time. He can move to a new neighborhood even though he has lived in the same house for thirty years. And he can take up a new hobby even though he is eighty years old.

Outer-directed people are often rigid because they put a great deal of emphasis on externals. For example, an outer-directed person will say, "He made me unhappy," whereas an inner-directed person will say, "I allowed myself to become unhappy." Outer-directed people are rigid because so much is riding on externals being a certain way. The rigidity stems from the need to control events that, in fact, they have no control over.

If you believe that other people make you unhappy, you are under constant pressure to have other people behave in certain ways. You are constantly at the mercy of factors outside yourself—over which you have little or no actual control. Inner-directed people know that they are responsible for the way they respond and feel—therefore the pressure that outer-directed people feel is nonexistent for them.

The reason that outer-directed people don't see an inner truth is because their attention is on things external to themselves—what other people think and do, what's wrong with the world, and so forth. As an outer-directed person allows himself to become more inner-directed, his attention is taken off events and occurrences that he has no control over—and put on his inner truth.

Outer-directed people do the same thing over and over again, giving such reasons as "I've always done it that way," "That's my nature," "That's the way it's done." Outer-directed people have a difficult time with change because change implies that there is no longer a preset way to do something.

At the very heart of inner-directed people lies the ability to be flexible. When a new truth emerges, they gravitate toward it. An inner-directed person who no longer loves her career, for example, will either find a new career that she does love, or will find a way to love her work again. An outer-directed person, on the other hand, will simply complain about her job and will likely do nothing constructive about it.

Many people inappropriately associate an inner-directed

person's capacity to change direction at a moment's notice with unreliability. They believe that if you say you're going to do something you must always follow through. The truth is, however, that a nonspontaneous person is, for the most part, far more unreliable than a spontaneous one. A person who is not spontaneous is also nonresponsive to what is going on at the moment. This, of course, has been a perpetual criticism of bureaucrats. The frustration of dealing with a bureaucrat, in the traditional sense of the word, is that he or she is unable to respond to the facts as they are *right now;* instead, the bureaucrat follows a narrow, rigid, and formal routine characterized by adherence to fixed rules and regulations. Instead of coming up with a spontaneous solution to a problem, bureaucrats often make excuses, saying, "That's the way things are supposed to be done." If a bureaucrat could become more inner-directed, he or she would be able to see simple solutions, usually requiring very little effort, that would assist a great number of people. The change, however, from outer to inner direction will not come from "the system"; it must come from within each individual.

A client, Ben, was a very outer-directed person. He was an interior designer of office space. One of his habits was comparing himself with others, particularly at work. He would design an office, then look at what one of his co-workers was doing, get frustrated, and start over. He couldn't stop comparing his work with others and believing that theirs was better. He came to me because it was becoming increasingly difficult for him to perform his duties. He felt extremely frustrated, and so did his boss!

His habit was so ingrained that most of the time he wasn't aware of it. Our sessions were geared toward getting Ben to become less outer-directed. The way we went about this was to make a game out of Ben's catching himself in the act as he began his habitual comparison. One thing he did know was how it felt to be actively engaged in his habit—it felt stressful. The feeling of stress was, in fact, quite different from other stress he felt. It was stronger and made him feel ashamed.

He learned to pay attention to the way he was feeling. When he felt the stress as he began to compare himself to others, he would say something silly to himself like, "Whoops, there I go again comparing myself to others." His goal was to catch himself earlier in the process. Just as it's easier to stop a snowball from rolling downhill when it's still relatively small, it's easier to stop any mental habit before it grows into a full-blown thought attack.

Eventually, Ben got so proficient at this game that he was able to catch himself preparing to compare, generating the thoughts that might lead to a comparison attack (as he learned to call it).

As you read through the remaining principles of happiness in this book, you'll notice that each of them stems from a strong sense of inner direction and the decision to take personal responsibility for your own happiness. This first principle, "Make yourself happy," is the foundation for all the others. As you commit to making yourself happy, you'll find that the remaining principles of happiness will quickly fall into place.

PRINCIPLE TWO:
Move with Your Moods

Time cools, time clarifies; no mood can be maintained quite unaltered through the course of hours.

—THOMAS MANN

One of the most important things to understand if you wish to move quickly through therapy is the distinction between real problems and mood-related problems. Obviously we have many significant problems and issues to contend with in our lives. However, the way we experience our personal problems can be very much affected by our mood when a difficult issue presents itself.

Moods are a fact of life. Sometimes you're in a high mood, other times you're in a lower mood. Many times you're somewhere in the middle. Luckily, high and low moods have very distinct, predictable characteristics that you can learn to be aware of.

When you're in a high mood life generally looks very good. You have a sense of lightness. You don't take anything too seriously. You feel happy, secure, patient, and confident. Your friends look like good people, your partner seems loving, your children and parents are wonderful. You feel fortunate to have a family. When you think of your life as a whole, you feel grateful, even lucky to be alive. Simple things intrigue you and you're easily satisfied.

When a problem presents itself while you're in a high mood, you deal with it the best you can. Solutions seem readily available, your creativity kicks in, and you feel excited about solving the problem. You're confident that a good solution will surface—that it's only a matter of time. When you think of your job or career, you think of its positive aspects; you're grateful you have a job or career. Life seems okay.

When you're in a lower mood, everything seems difficult. You're unhappy, insecure, impatient, defensive, irritable, and clumsy. When you think of your relationships while you're in a low mood they seem bothersome, shallow, and filled with problems. Your friends seem like strangers and their weaknesses glare. Your family seems dysfunctional and nonsupportive. You're easily bored and nothing seems to satisfy you. When a problem develops, it seems like the tip of the iceberg, as though more trouble is just around the corner. It looks as if there are no solutions. You feel hopeless. You have no creativity, wisdom, or common sense. Most of all, life seems to be one big emergency.

Almost all of our personal problems and difficult issues are very closely related to the mood we happen to be in when the issue presents itself.

Moods are part of the human condition. No one is immune to this part of emotional life. Luckily, however, you can come to understand your moods. You can learn to make very clear and deliberate allowances for the mood you're in. You can learn that while in lower moods, you can't trust yourself. Your judgment is faulty. The decisions you make will always be less than ideal, even laughable, and if you act on them you'll likely wish you hadn't.

You can learn to predict how you're going to react to life

while you are in certain moods, thus protecting yourself from the deceptive nature of your own moods.

Expect Your Moods to Change Constantly

Surprisingly, very few people (including many therapists) realize that moods are always changing, thus altering the way we feel about the issues in our lives. How many times have you thought one day that your life was wonderful—and the next thought it was horrible? How often has your job seemed rewarding before lunch and distasteful after lunch? Isn't it true that your partner sometimes seems loving one minute and critical the next? These and endless other examples are explained by moods. Your life, your job, your mate, your children, don't really change much from moment to moment. What does change is the way you *feel*—your mood. As your mood drops, every part of your life looks worse than it really is. The lower the mood, the gloomier it looks. And to make matters worse, everything you see while you're feeling low seems to justify the way you're feeling. It's almost as though you put up an invisible negative antenna encouraging you to notice everything that's wrong with your life.

A client recently told me that he absolutely loved his job. He raved about his challenging responsibilities, his terrific pay and benefits, and his understanding boss. Clearly he was in a high mood. The very next week he approached me looking as if he had lost his best friend. His face was drawn. He explained that his problem was his "boring job." He went on to say that he had no important responsibilities, his boss was a tyrant, and he was underpaid and unappreciated.

"Am I wrong, or weren't you just telling me about how wonderful your job was?" I asked.

His reply: "I was fooling myself like I always do. My job is the pits. I hate it."

Such a drastic turnaround may on the surface seem ridiculous, but we all do this, to different degrees. When we feel good, life looks good. When we feel bad, life looks bad. It's that simple. When you understand the powerful deceptive nature of low moods, you'll see how this client's opposing ways of viewing his job were quite predictable.

Defend Yourself from a Mood Attack

Although a low mood is certainly no fun, the mood itself isn't the real problem. The problem is what you decide to do with it. If you're in a low mood and you don't overreact, you can easily maintain your perspective by making certain allowances for the way you're currently feeling. If you know you're low and seeing life negatively, you are, in a real sense, protected from yourself. Your understanding of moods allows you to take action based entirely on how you feel. You know you should wait until you feel better, when your wisdom will resurface, to act or make important decisions.

If you trust in the way you're feeling and act on your negative feelings, you're going to be in serious trouble. Think about it: How much wisdom do you have in your lowest states of mind? How much compassion do you feel for others when you're angry or depressed? How much common sense do you have available to you when you're feeling bad? Very little. Doesn't life always look better and seem easier when you feel good?

What if you knew in advance that any action you took or decision you made would be counterproductive? Would you still take action? Would you still make the decision? Of course not. When you understand moods, despite the urgency you feel, you won't act when you're feeling low.

Being aware of the predictable characteristics of your low moods allows you to know in advance exactly what to expect— and this makes life much easier. In a low mood you can expect to feel anger toward your spouse, you can expect to think negatively about your marriage, and you can expect to be pessimistic about your future. But if you know these feelings are going to crop up every single time you're low, aren't you, in a sense, protected? Can't you, with this information, take yourself a little less seriously?

Life is more predictable when you're prepared for bad moods. The next time you feel gloomy, you can say to yourself, "Of course I'm going to be thinking like this. I always think like this when I'm low. I know that nothing is really as bad as it seems right now." Won't that understanding give you hope? It should, because it's correct 100 percent of the time.

Be on the Lookout for Your Low Moods in Therapy

When a therapist asks you to explain how you're feeling or what you're thinking about—what is he or she really asking you? Isn't the therapist usually trying to get you to explain the way you see life and your problems *when you're feeling low?*

Does your therapist ever remind you that your life only looks this way while you're feeling the way you are right now—while you're feeling low? Remember, an hour from now, or tomorrow, when you're in a better state, when your mood is higher, it's very likely, almost certain, that you will see the same set of facts entirely differently. "How do you feel?" is an extremely relative question. The honest answer is "It depends." Are you in a secure, forgiving, positive state of mind—a state of mind in which you're capable of learning and growing? Or are you in a negative, pessimistic, low state of mind?

> *If you're in a low mood and you don't overreact, you can quite easily maintain your perspective by making certain allowances for the way you're feeling.*

The emphasis in therapy is very often on the most negative parts of your life. But if all aspects of life, all of the time, look awful when you're feeling low, why bother trying to explain the details and specifics regarding the way you're feeling? Couldn't this be looked at as a waste of time? If you're feeling bad about something, continuing to discuss it while you're still feeling bad is an endless cycle. The fact that you feel low fuels the bad feelings further. This is called a negative spiral. Certainly one therapy session consisting of talking through your negative feelings isn't going to solve your problem, so you'd better come back next week!

But the most significant part of this dilemma isn't the problem itself; it's all the attention you give to the situation when you feel low. In terms of getting through therapy quickly, the most relevant issue is never the issue itself, but your state of mind when you talk about it.

Even if you were to "figure out" the reasons behind the problems in your life, often a goal of therapy, the very next time you fell into a low mood, your life would look just as bad to you as it did before you figured everything out. This means that you could spend the rest of your life in therapy confusing real problems with mood-related problems. Obviously this would be prohibitively expensive. It would also be unnecessary. Every time something went wrong with your life, rather than seeing how your mood was contributing to the way you were feeling, you would bring up the issue with your therapist. If your therapist didn't understand the concept of low and high moods, he or she would be inclined to discuss the problem with you as if the problem itself were what made you feel bad. But the problem, regardless of what it is, will look drastically different to you depending on the mood you happen to be in.

If, instead of focusing on your problems, your therapist could teach you the role your own moods play in your perception of your problems, you would have a useful, practical tool to use whenever a problem emerged in your life, whatever it happened to be.

Quite a bit of therapy is spent in remembering, analyzing, and rehashing your past. Is this useful? I suppose it can be. But again, the mood you're in while you're thinking about your past will determine how you interpret what you remember.

A fascinating thing to do is to ask a close friend to discuss his past with you while he is in a very low mood. Then do the very same thing while he's in a happy, contented mood. You may be shocked. It will seem as if your friend had two different pasts, not in details and facts, but in his experience of them.

A client of mine remembered in a low mood that her parents didn't allow her to attend summer camp. She was angry and resentful. Her previous therapist had encouraged her to "get into" this memory—as if doing so would help her. She remembered her humiliation and that she wanted to run away. She said she hated her parents.

One day, while she was in a very good mood, I encouraged her to remember the same incident. Guess what? She recalled that the reason her parents didn't send her to summer camp was that they simply couldn't afford to. Furthermore, instead of sending her to camp, they gave her swimming lessons at the YMCA. It was during those lessons that she met her best-ever, lifelong friend, the person who later became her bridesmaid. While my client was feeling good, the same memory had an entirely different cast. She felt compassion and understanding for her parents and was grateful for the friend she had met.

I'm not suggesting there is never any value in remembering painful events in your life. It's important, however, to keep in mind that your mood will play a key role in what you happen to remember and in your experience of that memory.

Again, the reason this is so critical to speeding through therapy is that without an understanding of moods, you could spend years thinking about your painful past, never realizing the role your current mood is playing in your perceptions. Once you understand this, you can gain a perspective on your past that allows you to move on toward your future.

When's a Good Time to Talk About Your Problems?

I was working with a married couple who felt their marriage was stressful. When I asked them to think about the time they usually discussed their problems, their reply was "Whenever we feel stressed out, we talk about it." When I suggested that they do just the opposite, that they wait until they feel relaxed to discuss their problems, they said: "But if we waited until we felt relaxed, we wouldn't perceive that we had any problems." This was exactly the point I was trying to get them to see. Many, if not most, problems only appear to be problems when you're feeling bad. If you can cultivate the patience and wisdom to leave your problems alone as much as possible when you're feeling negative, and try not to discuss or figure anything out when you're low, you'll usually discover what these clients did: Problems are a function of the way you feel. Getting into them while you feel negative only makes them seem worse.

Take note of your mood. Do you feel secure and peaceful? Or do you feel uncomfortable and unsettled? It doesn't ultimately matter whether you feel good or bad at this particular moment, but it's *critical* that you be at least aware of how you feel. If you feel good, if your mood is relatively high, if you feel open, receptive, trusting, and nondefensive, you can trust that your perspective will be quite keen. This is an excellent time to ponder your life and discuss issues. If you have a problem, go ahead and solve it.

Many people who hear about this concept of moods immediately recognize its wisdom and common sense. They instinctively understand that it's not in their best interest to think about their problems and shortcomings while they don't feel well emotionally. So why do they still get caught up in problem solving during low moods?

The answer is very simple. Every time you feel *any* emotion associated with a low mood—depression, anger, stress, frustration, jealousy, insecurity—you're going to feel tempted to try to think your way out of it.

As we have been discussing, inherent in any low mood is a sense of urgency, the need to get away from how you're feeling. The unfortunate result is that people have most of their serious discussions about important topics—children, money, sex, romance, careers—when they feel low and hopeless, when they are least equipped to do so. As sad as this is, it makes complete sense. After all, you rarely feel like discussing a relationship problem when you're not feeling angry. But again, that's the whole point of this discussion: If you can wait until you don't feel the negative feelings to discuss them, most of them will vanish. Rest assured, if you have a legitimate gripe, concern, or problem in a low mood, it will still be there when your mood rises and you are far better equipped to deal with it.

Where Do Your Moods Go?

The secret of overcoming the compelling negative delusions of moods is to be assured that moods will come and go as long as you leave them alone. All moods, even the painfully black ones, are fueled and exacerbated by only one thing: your thinking. The more thought and discussion you indulge in about why you feel the way you do, the longer your low mood will last. The more attention you give to your low mood, and the more you try to fight it and figure it out, the worse it will seem and the longer it will last. If you can just relax and remember that your mood will pass, if you can somehow leave it alone, your mood will rise before you know it. You'll be back to your higher-mood self. Be patient. Trust in the movement of moods. You've had thousands of low moods and every single one of them has vanished.

> *Your mood is the source of your experience, not the effect.*

You now see that your mood affects every aspect of your life, including the way you interpret your life while speaking to your therapist. If you feel hopeful and loving while you speak to your therapist, you'll see a bright future. If you feel bitter and resentful, the future you see will be dark. As you begin to pay more attention to the mood you're in and less attention to thinking about, discussing, and solving your problems while you're feeling low, you'll begin to understand this shortcut through therapy.

PRINCIPLE THREE:
Think Your Thoughts—
Let Them Go

*There is nothing either good or bad, but
thinking makes it so.*

—SHAKESPEARE, *HAMLET*

Without question, thought is my favorite shortcut through
therapy. Discovering the ways your thoughts can emotionally
hurt or help you is exciting and important. I have known hundreds of people who turned their lives around when they
understood the role thought played in their emotional experience. One of the most gratifying aspects of this discovery is
that many of these turnarounds occur quickly, without too
much effort.

If there is one certainty, it's that we think. Every moment
of every day, our minds are busy trying to make sense out of
life. We think about our past, our present, our future. We
worry and contemplate. We remember. We have guilty
thoughts, thoughts of shame, pessimism and optimism. Forever busy, our thinking minds attempt to figure out life and
solve our problems.

Your Feelings Come from the Thoughts You Think

Simply put, your feelings are caused by the thoughts you're thinking. You can't feel sad without first having sad thoughts, be angry without angry thoughts, or be frustrated without first thinking about what's frustrating you. If you were going to get yourself all worked up, how would you do it? There's only one way. You'd have to think about something that bothered you to feel the corresponding emotion. Pretty obvious, isn't it?

But this obvious link between thinking and feeling is little understood. Very few people live their lives as if they comprehend this basic truth, and sadly this includes most mental-health professionals. Many mental-health workers actually encourage clients to think *exclusively* about the things that make them sad and angry, and then wonder why their clients never seem to feel better.

Thinking about something can take up an extended period, or only a moment. In either case, the valid relationship between thinking and feeling exists. If you have the thought, even in passing, "I always feel depressed on Mondays," the fact that you now feel low on Monday is not a coincidence. If you have the thought "You can't really bypass therapy by reading a book," the fact that you now feel a little skeptical came about the same instant you had that thought.

Many therapists who don't understand the link between thoughts and feelings would respond to the statement "I always feel depressed on Mondays" by automatically asking you to explain further. In doing so, a therapist would in effect be saying, "Okay, that thought made you feel bad. Can you create some additional thoughts along the same lines so you can feel even worse?"

A good starting point toward understanding the nature of thought is to ask yourself this question: "If negative thoughts make me feel bad, what's the sense of intentionally creating even more of them?" As we move on in this chapter, it will become very clear what a therapist might ask you instead of suggesting that you dwell on your negative thoughts. In fact, we'll return to this specific example later on.

The ill effects of thought come about when we forget that we are the producers of our own thoughts. Thought isn't something that happens *to* us, but something we are doing, from the inside. Once we understand that we are the producers of our own thinking, and that our thoughts create, moment to moment, the way we feel, paying too much attention to our negative thoughts or taking them too seriously begins to lose its appeal.

> *It's our thinking about our circumstances, not the circumstances themselves, that determines how we feel.*

Consider the business professional who, after twenty successful years, has a string of bad luck and is forced into bankruptcy. Ten years later she is on her feet again, though not at the same level as before. Every now and then she remembers her mistakes, and somehow she can never completely let go of the past. She enters therapy with a drawn face and explains that she is very depressed. When asked why, she tells the story of her business failure.

This woman, a rather typical client, came to my stress management center to get away from her stress. Initially she didn't see herself as the thinker of her own thoughts, nor did she believe that her thoughts created her misery. In fact, when I suggested that her thoughts were making her depressed, she responded, "My thoughts have nothing to do with the way I feel. The reason I'm so upset is because I blew a fortune and was forced into bankruptcy."

I could substitute a hundred examples for this one. Whether it's a string of bad luck, a painful past, an uncertain future, or a difficult marriage—it's all the same. It's our thinking about our circumstances, not the circumstances themselves, that determines how we feel. In the absence of thoughts about "what's wrong," the ill feelings disappear, even if the circumstance remains. In other words, your life on an external level may not improve, but without a focus of thought on a particular circumstance, a negative feeling *cannot* exist. When we lose sight of the fact that *we* are the ones doing the thinking that upsets us, it can appear as though our circumstances create our feelings. This encourages us to blame our unhappiness on our circumstances. The sad result of this misunderstanding is a feeling of powerlessness.

To believe that your circumstances, and not your thinking, are the ultimate cause of any unhappiness you suffer is a serious mistake with far-reaching negative consequences. What would happen if all your dreams came true and your external life looked perfect? Sounds great, doesn't it? But what if the one hitch was that you continued to think negatively about life? I can tell you with absolute certainty that you'd be every bit as miserable as before. I've had many clients who said to me, "I don't know what's wrong. I have everything—money, fame, great children, a good marriage, a beautiful home, a promising future. But I feel terrible. What's wrong?"

Most people fill their minds with negativity without realizing it—and without understanding the effect this negativity has on their own well-being. Sometimes people who seem to have everything are even more unhappy than those who have virtually nothing. They are so convinced that circumstances determine personal happiness that they have completely forgotten the role that their own thinking plays in their life.

On the reverse side, I've seen many people who seemingly have very difficult lives, yet have learned to stop exacerbating their problems and making themselves feel bad with their own thinking. Many people with exceptionally serious problems have learned that the secret of personal contentment has little to do with the way their life looks on the outside, and a great deal to do with their relationship to their own thinking. They have learned that thinking is an ability, not a reality—and that thoughts do not have to be taken so seriously.

How to Think Yourself into a State of Mind

It's easy to allow our own thinking to upset us and take us away from where we want to be emotionally. Allow me to share a personal example.

Because I have a stress management practice to run, a family to raise, and a generally busy schedule, one of the best times for me to write is in the wee hours of the morning—three to six a.m. The children are sleeping (usually) and the phone rarely rings. One morning I woke up very excited because I had what I considered some excellent ideas to add to this book.

About the time I sat down at my computer and poured myself a cup of coffee, my youngest daughter woke up in her crib and began talking and crying. "Oh no, not now" was my initial thought. Usually the baby goes right back to sleep, but that day she stayed awake—the noise didn't stop. I went in a few times to hold her and quiet her down, but to no avail. Each time I'd sit down at my computer, she'd start up again.

My thoughts were rapidly forming into something like this: "Every time I try to get some quiet around here, someone interrupts me. It's no use to work at home; I should reserve more time at the office. Kids are so difficult," and so forth. An hour earlier I'd been excited to be alive and eager to write. Now I was upset, feeling like a victim, and generally frustrated. And even though I spend the better part of each day teaching people otherwise, I honestly felt as though someone else—my daughter—was responsible for the way I was feeling.

Luckily, it didn't last too long. About an hour later, I suddenly realized what I was doing to myself. I was allowing my thoughts to run wild. I was paying so much attention to my thoughts of frustration that I was allowing them to lower my spirits and my state of mind.

Most of us do the same thing many times a day. We think about something (it could be anything) and believe that the object of our thoughts is responsible for the lowering of our spirits. It isn't. Whenever we have a thought, or a series of thoughts, and believe them to be true, we'll feel the effect of those thoughts. In other words, the act of thinking, and not the object of our thinking, is responsible for our state of mind. Another way of saying this is that the act of getting caught up in a situation is more relevant than what we're caught up in.

In this example, the circumstance I was in (being interrupted) was neutral. It simply was what it was. The act of thinking about my circumstance, and its effects on what I wanted to be doing, was the factor that was creating my state of mind. Had my attention been on something else, I wouldn't have felt bad at all. I had temporarily lost sight of the fact that *I* was the one who was doing the thinking. It was as if I were banging my head against a wall without realizing I was doing the banging—and then blaming the wall for the pain.

Here's another example. Katie was stressed because her hours at work were, in her words, "far too many." She felt she was wasting her life at the office and had no time to enjoy herself. Initially, when I discussed with her the important relationship between her thinking and the way she was feeling, she politely responded that although she understood what I was talking about, this relationship "wasn't relevant" to her situation.

I asked her how much time she guessed she spent thinking about the number of hours she was working—during the hours she *wasn't* working. Her first response was "no time at all."

"Didn't you just spend a half hour telling me about how many hours you work?" I asked.

"Well, yes, but that's different," she said. "I had to tell you my problem, didn't I?"

"Perhaps you did," I responded, "but *the way you feel* about the number of hours you work is more related to the *fact that you are thinking* about this issue than it is to the number of hours you actually spend working." She seemed curious, so I continued. "It's true that you work a great number of hours, and perhaps that can be changed, but the real issue here is how you feel about the time you spend working, isn't it?"

"Yes, of course."

"Well, how do you feel about the number of hours you work when you're holding your baby boy in your arms and gazing into his eyes?" I asked.

"It's irrelevant at that moment because I'm busy doing something else more important," she responded.

"But the fact that you spend a lot of time working is still true. Am I right?"

"Yes. What are you getting at?"

"You were visibly upset while you were telling me about the number of hours you spend working, yet you say you aren't upset by the same set of facts while you're doing something you enjoy. Does this tell you something?"

"It tells me that I'm only upset about my life while I'm actively thinking about an issue."

"Exactly," I said.

Katie looked at me with a very puzzled expression and said, "You know, now that I think about it, I spend most of my time away from work thinking about how much time I'm at work— and those are precisely the times I feel overwhelmed." Five minutes earlier she had said she spent no time at all thinking about this issue.

The specific details of the things you think about aren't as important to the way you're feeling as is the fact that you're thinking about them. In other words, had Katie been busy thinking, not about how long her hours at the office were, but about how difficult it is to be a working mother, or how unfortunate it was that she was gaining weight, her internal process would have been identical in terms of getting herself upset. During those moments when she *wasn't* thinking about this issue, it wouldn't have been bothering her. Again, the fact that you're caught up in your thinking is more relevant to the way you're feeling than are the specifics of what you happen to be caught up in.

During our next session, Katie had an insight about her life that is worth repeating here: "I've realized that I haven't been wasting my life at the office, but that I have been wasting my life thinking about how much time I spend at the office!"

Seeing the look in her eyes when she said this assured me that this would be less of an issue in her life. The state of mind Katie would be living in from this point forth would be generally higher than it had been. Therefore any decision to cut back her hours, or even change her job or her way of living, would be made easily.

All of us are at our personal best, with the greatest access to our wisdom and common sense, when our minds are free from negative distractions. The peaceful state of mind that comes about from an understanding of the role of your own thinking, enables you to make wise decisions that support your goals and needs. In an upset or frantic state of mind, just the opposite is likely to happen. If an answer can't be found while you're in a positive state of mind, it's highly unlikely that an answer can be found at all.

Catch Yourself Thinking

On the surface, it looked as though Katie's problem was all about the number of hours she was working and how to change that. She said her previous therapist had spent their entire time (once a week for a whole year) discussing this issue and how it made her feel. After fifty sessions, Katie felt worse than before she had started therapy and was no closer to making any changes.

> *Once you see that your thoughts cause your negative feelings, you can watch yourself creating your own misery.*

The deeper issue (as it always is) was Katie's lack of awareness that she was, in fact, thinking about the issue way too much—and on an even deeper level, she was completely un-aware of the effect this thinking was having on her life. When looked at from this broader, deeper perspective, the solution was simple. Katie needed to learn to catch herself thinking about the issue and to dismiss the thoughts from her mind.

An additional insight freed Katie even further. She became angry at her previous therapist for keeping her in therapy for so long without results. She started saying things like "What a crook," and "She doesn't deserve to work with people."

"Just a minute," I said. "Do you see what you're doing right now?"

"Oh my gosh," she said, "I can't believe it. Even after real-izing that my thinking is what upsets me, I forget for just a moment and start doing it again."

Katie had a thought about something (her previous thera-pist), and rather than recognizing it as just a thought, she be-gan taking it seriously, getting all upset, blaming her therapist, and starting the entire cycle all over again. It's easy to do even when you realize what you're doing.

We tend to believe that the source of our upset is what we're thinking about. If, for example, you had an argument with your husband an hour ago and are still thinking about it right now, it will seem as though your husband, not your thoughts about your husband, is making you angry or frus-trated. But this isn't so. It's true you had the argument, and it might even be the case that the two of you need to work on some component of your relationship, *but that is an entirely dif-ferent issue.* What we're talking about here is the reason you're feeling bad. The cause of your negative feelings is *the fact that you're thinking about an incident that is over.*

The same was true when I wasn't able to get any writing done at four o'clock in the morning. Yes, my daughter played a part in my inability to write, but the cause of my negative feelings wasn't my eighteen-month-old daughter, it was my thoughts about the incident and my lack of awareness about being caught up in my thinking.

Once you see this distinction, you are empowered to do

something about your frustrations in life. Once you see that your thoughts cause your negative feelings, you can watch yourself creating your own misery. When you catch yourself thinking your way into a negative state of mind, it's pretty simple to stop doing so.

Take Action

I have frequently been asked, "Are you suggesting that I don't take action?" Absolutely not. In fact, when you fully understand the role your own thinking plays in upsetting you, action becomes much easier.

Let's return to my daughter's interruption of my work. If I were to remain frustrated about this incident, continuing to think about the issue, I'd increase this frustration each time a similar thing happened, and my spirits would be low. My ability to think through my needs with a clear mind and to take action would be limited. Chances are I would spend time and energy complaining and feeling like a victim instead of writing. I would discuss my frustration with my wife, my friends, or even a therapist and keep the issue alive in my mind. In all likelihood, I would make no positive changes, but would probably repeat any mistakes I was making. If I paid too much attention to my thoughts and took them too seriously, I could end up resenting my daughter.

However, once I see that my own thinking is creating my negative feelings, new options appear instantly. I can quickly choose not to be upset about the interruption. I can remind myself that this is a risk I take by working at home. Or I can calmly decide to make different decisions regarding when and where I do my writing. Either way, I avoid unnecessary frustration. I'm now in charge of the way I am feeling; my daughter isn't.

Many of us have certain things that we feel we simply *can't* stop thinking about. As your understanding of the relationship between thought and feeling deepens, you will discover that this needn't be true.

It's extremely difficult to stop thinking about a pressing issue in your life whenever you believe it's solely responsible for the way you feel. If you believe your employer is making you miserable, it will be difficult to stop thinking about her. However, if you understand that it is your thoughts about your employer that upset you, then as those thoughts drift into your mind, it's fairly easy to dismiss them. When you realize your thoughts have no power to hurt you, they will seem less significant, regardless of their content. Whenever something seems less significant, letting it go seems easier and more reasonable.

You Think Thoughts, Not Reality

Thinking is an ability, a function of human consciousness. It is something we do, not something that happens to us. If we forget this important fact, we may innocently interpret our thoughts as if they were reality, as if their presence in our mind means they are true and all-important and must be attended to.

Our thoughts are real thoughts, but that's all they are. When we recognize this, we are able to dismiss or ignore negative thoughts that pass through our minds. As we do, positive feelings begin to emerge. However, if we believe our thoughts are reality, if we harbor our negative thoughts and pay too much attention to them, we will lose this positive feeling and feel the effects of the negativity.

Suppose you're driving in your car and someone accidentally swerves into your lane, almost causing an accident. You look over expecting to see the person wave an apologetic hand. Instead, he yells an obscenity at you and drives away. You are enraged. "What's the matter with that jerk?" you think to yourself. "I can't believe some people." Your thoughts about the incident make you even more frustrated and you spend the entire morning thinking about it. Every time you think about it, you feel angry again. After work you drive home and call a friend. You tell her about the incident, which encourages you to think about it even more. Your head is filled with negativity and you feel frustrated.

The actual incident was unfortunate but only lasted about ten seconds. Furthermore, no one was injured, nor was any damage done. But your negative feelings continue throughout the day and perhaps even longer.

The trick in becoming less a victim of your own thinking is to remember that *you* are the thinker who is filling your head with negative thoughts. As you think about something, you'll feel the effects of your thoughts. Once you understand and feel this important fact, you'll be able to catch yourself filling your head with negativity. You'll realize that despite what it may have looked like at the scene of the near accident, it was your thoughts, not the driver who almost hit you, that ruined your day.

When you can master the implications of this important distinction your life will begin to improve immediately. When you see the logic and ease in ceasing to follow every negative train of thought that comes into your head, a more positive feeling will begin to emerge. Random thoughts may continue to fill your head, but as long as you view them as just thoughts, their negative impact on you will be minimal. In the above example, a thought like "That driver was such a jerk" entered your mind. But instead of following that thought with another negative thought, you can say to yourself, "Silly me, there I go again upsetting myself with more negative thoughts." We have limited control over events, but we have complete control over whether we allow our own thoughts to upset us.

Pick and Choose Your Thoughts

You may be surprised at how often you entertain a negative thought or series of negative thoughts without even realizing you're doing so. When you have a negative thought, it's entirely up to you what you do with it. It all depends on your relationship to your own thinking. Do you believe you think thoughts, or do you believe you think reality?

When a negative thought enters your mind, you can analyze that thought, or you can dismiss it.

Suppose you have the thought "I could never learn to play tennis." What now? You can do one of two things. You can believe your thought, considering it a reality that you could never learn to play tennis. After all, you created that thought. Or you can view this thought merely as a thought. It's not a big deal! You can dismiss it. You'll have thousands of other thoughts today as well.

One of the questions I'm most frequently asked is "If my thoughts aren't real, how do I know which ones to pay attention to?" The best way to answer this question is with another question: "Does this thought serve me?" If you're ever unsure whether to believe a thought and take it seriously, apply this simple test.

Thought is a gift, a powerful tool of the mind—a tool to help us organize, sift through, and make sense out of life. But not all thoughts are sacred or need to be entertained. Many are based on fear, defensiveness, and extreme pessimism. It's critical to remember that your thoughts are mood-related.

Thoughts stemming from a low mood are going to be damaging, lacking wisdom and perspective.

The thoughts you create in a low mood will usually make no sense whatsoever. Often you'll look back on those thoughts when your mood rises and wonder how you could ever have thought such things. Your dark and meaningless life as seen through a low mood will appear bright, hopeful, and important as soon as your mood rises.

The thoughts you should pay attention to are the thoughts that brighten your spirits.

Pay attention to the thoughts that are based on wisdom, gratitude, perspective, and common sense. Ignore those grounded in a low, pessimistic mood—thoughts of gloom and doom, fear, lack of appreciation, hopelessness, despair, negativity, and anger.

The way to tell whether you're paying attention to the right thoughts is by the way you feel. You feel the way you think. If you're feeling low, this tells you that you're thinking in ways that don't serve you—you can be certain your thinking is negative and should be ignored. Conversely, if you're feeling good, you know your thinking is functional. It's doing what it's supposed to do.

Isn't This Denial?

Absolutely not! Denial means refusal to acknowledge. When you understand the role thought plays in your life, you do just the opposite. You acknowledge the act of your own thinking. You also acknowledge the powerful connection between your thoughts and the way you feel. In fact, in giving so much credit to this connection, you consciously choose to ignore those thoughts that take you away from what it is you're looking for—contentment.

Suppose you're thirty-eight years old and the thought passes through your mind, "My mother had a lot of problems when I was a kid. She drank too much and at times she was verbally abusive." Further, suppose this thought is depressing you or making you angry and you choose to dismiss it. That's not denial. Here's denial: "My mother was perfect. We didn't have any problems. Our family was ideal." Denial is trying to pretend or convince yourself that life is other than it really is, was, or is going to be. But the greater wisdom, in this case, would be to choose to dismiss the thoughts you had about your mother, not because you deny the facts, but because you're paying attention to the way you're feeling—depressed or angry—and that's not the way you wish to feel. You know that if you don't pay too much attention to this thought about your mother, it won't bother you.

Your thoughts make you angry; your past does not.

"But it's important to acknowledge that your relationship to your mother bothers you," some therapists will insist. This insistence is ignorant of the fact that it's your thinking, not your past circumstances, that "bothers" you. *Any time* you have a thought, and believe that thought to be true, it will bother you. *This* is the fact it's important to acknowledge. Your relationship to your mother bothers you only while you're thinking about it. Encouraging someone to think about something simply to prove the fact that it will bother him or her is outrageous. Of course it will. Again, what bothers you isn't your relationship, but the effects of your own thoughts about the relationship.

Know that once you establish an understanding of the role thought plays in your life to keep you unhappy, you're free to think about anything you like. Once you cease to allow your own thinking to destroy your well-being, you can think all you wish about the relationship you had with your mother when you were a child. The difference will be that you won't become upset every time you do so. And while this may bother some therapists who are stuck on the idea that anyone who thinks about a painful past without becoming angry is in denial, you can rest assured that this isn't truc.

When people realize that they have control over the way they feel, they feel relieved and finally become interested in their own past rather than being frightened or angered by it. They realize that their past, while real at the time, is now only a thought that is being carried through time via their own mind. Nothing more, nothing less.

Many therapists insist that it's important to allow yourself to become angry in the present because you weren't allowed that privilege when you were a child. Again, it's important to remember what you're really getting angry about. If you want to acknowledge the imperfections of your childhood and achieve crystal clarity about the way things really were, go right ahead. But the best way to do this isn't through arguing for your right to be angry. The most effective way to learn about your past is to develop a compassionate attitude—sometimes called forgiveness—toward past events and experiences. And the first step is to understand the difference between thought and reality.

Don't Attach Too Much Importance to Your Thoughts

If you wrote yourself a mean-spirited letter—would you be offended by that letter? Of course you wouldn't, but why?

You would be completely aware that *you* were the one who wrote the letter. This recognition would be your protection against self-sabotage. Similarly, you wouldn't yell, "Boo" and be frightened by your own voice. Again, your knowledge of the fact that you, not someone else were the responsible party, protects you from unnecessary mental anguish and fear.

You Can Learn to See That Your Own Thoughts Are Causing You to Feel Overwhelmed and Stressed

Most of us are capable of having a thought like "My life is no good" and then feeling depressed or hopeless by virtue of taking this thought too seriously.

Remember that your thinking is to the way you feel the way a clip of film is to what you see on the screen at a movie theater. Just as you wouldn't bring a rifle to shoot a monster you saw on the screen, you can learn to relate to your thinking in a similar manner. You don't need to react to, take seriously, or even be all that interested in the thoughts you're having at the moment. You can see your thoughts—as thoughts. They will enter your mind and they will leave. The less importance you attach to any particular thought, the less impact that thought will have on your well-being.

Suppose you're in the habit of rushing around as if life were one big emergency. You're constantly having thoughts validating your belief in the scarcity of time. You're in the car, running fifteen minutes late, thinking to yourself, "Oh no, I'm late again. What am I going to do?" Each time you find yourself in this familiar scenario, you're at a very important crossroads. If you pay attention to these thoughts and allow them to run their course, you're almost certainly going to feel rushed, frustrated, even overwhelmed.

What if, instead of paying so much attention to these thoughts, you suddenly realized, "Hey, here I go again. My mind's rushing." What if you also realized that your own thinking was contributing greatly to your feeling of stress? This recognition would help you slow down your thinking, which in turn would allow you to relax.

Whenever you observe your own mind working against itself, and simultaneously realize what you're doing to yourself, you immediately enable yourself to take another course of action. In the absence of those thoughts, you'll begin to feel better.

"But I really *am* running late," you might be thinking. What you must realize is that a frenzied mind isn't a more efficient mind—it certainly won't help you arrive at your destination any earlier. By learning to quiet down your mind and get a grip on your thinking, you reduce your internal level of stress, which enables you to maintain your perspective and wisdom. If you're late but your internal stress is low, you'll be better equipped to explain yourself to the person you're meeting. If you arrive frantic, you'll only create the appearance of an emergency and likely exacerbate any problems your lateness has created.

Take a Shortcut Through Therapy

Most of the emphasis in most types of therapy is on the content of what you happen to be thinking about. A shortcut through therapy is this: *The recognition of the fact that you're caught up in your own thinking is far more relevant than whatever you happen to be caught up in.*

As you sense the powerful connection between your thoughts and the way you feel—and as you gently put into practice your ability to let your thoughts go, you will be preparing yourself for the next principle. Whenever you are caught up in your own thinking—regardless of what you happen to be caught up about—your mind is too busy and full of concerns to see the more positive aspects of life. But, as your mind quiets down and becomes less absorbed with insecure thoughts, and as you begin to dismiss the negative thoughts that do enter your mind, you will naturally, without too much effort, begin focusing your attention on what's right with your life, the essence of principle number four. So, let's move on!

Principle Four:
Look for the Silver Lining

No pessimist ever discovered the secrets of the stars, or sailed to an uncharted land, or opened a new heaven to the human spirit.

—Helen Keller

As I sat down at my computer to begin writing this chapter, I received a phone call from my auto mechanic letting me know that my car needed twice the brake work the mechanic had originally thought, at twice the original estimate.

The question isn't whether we will be regularly faced with adversity. We most certainly will. The relevant question if you want to live a more effective life with less stress and more contentment is "How will I respond to this adversity?"

If I were a pessimist, after that phone call I'd probably have thought, "Mechanics are crooks," or something equally suspicious and negative. But being an optimist, I thought instead, "Oh well, at least the car will be safer, and perhaps the ride will be a little smoother."

If you're a pessimist, your negative thinking won't be limited to episodes such as disappointing news from your mechanic. If you're in the habit of negative thinking, chances are you'll almost always see the dark side of a situation. Whenever anything difficult happens in your life, irrespective of how minor it might be—your neighbor's yard isn't picked up to your satisfaction, your faucet begins leaking, or your child sneezes—you imagine the absolute worst: Your neighbor is being sloppy just to upset you; your apartment is falling apart; your child is about to come down with the measles. You also imagine that somehow you're responsible for these terrible occurrences, so you should now feel guilty or resentful.

> *Your thoughts ultimately determine the way you're going to feel.*

Each of the principles discussed in this book emphasizes, at least in part, the important relationship between your thoughts and your feelings. The way you feel plays a major role in determining your responses to events in your life—your behavior. In a practical sense, then, negative or pessimistic thinking does two things. First, it makes you feel bad, and second, it distorts your behavior.

Is a Cancelled Lunch Date the End of the World?

Let me give you an example of how your behavior can become distorted as a result of negative thinking. Suppose one of your best friends calls to cancel a lunch date. Rather than seeing the good side of this sudden change of plans, you react in a pessimistic fashion. You think to yourself, "She's always canceling on me. What good is she anyway? Who needs her?" Deep down, you may even mean these things, but your mind has produced these negative thoughts. Since your thinking determines the way you are going to feel, you are now feeling a little sorry for yourself, maybe a little self-righteous or angry. Ten minutes later you pick up the mail only to discover that the tickets you ordered to the local concert have arrived. You were going to invite your friend, Sally, but she's the one who always cancels on you—so you decide you're just going to forget about the show and give the tickets away!

At first glance this little scenario seems harmless enough—it's simply a reaction to some simple frustration, isn't it? Yes it is—but only in part. The truth is, your friend didn't cause your reaction, it was your thoughts about the cancellation that caused you to be upset. But now, because you failed to recognize this distinction, you have lost an opportunity to spend an evening with your best friend! And remember, what you thought you were upset about was the fact that you don't get to spend enough time with your friend.

It's easy to feel that you have the "right" to be angry or pessimistic. You certainly do, but you also have the "right" to have a heart attack or an auto accident, and you certainly don't want that! So often, negative, pessimistic thinking can creep insidiously into your mind, fueling the compelling urge to pay attention to those thoughts. Many experienced therapists, in fact, will insist that when you are negative you are merely being honest about your "true feelings," that you are getting in touch with your dark side—and that this is a really good idea! The truth is, getting in touch with your dark or negative side in this way will do only one thing for you—assist you in feeling sorry for yourself.

Do You Practice Being Unhappy?

You've learned that the act of thinking negatively is more relevant to any unhappiness you suffer than what you happen to be thinking about. What this means in a practical sense is this: When you think in a negative manner, you're actually practicing being unhappy. Think about it. Your thoughts determine the way you feel. A friend cancels a lunch date and you think something like "My friend doesn't like me anymore." These thoughts translate into the negative feelings associated with the thoughts—in this case, self-pity and sadness.

The tricky part of this understanding is that it always seems as though you have good reason to be upset. Your friend really did cancel the get-together you were looking forward to. It seems logical, at some level, that you feel bad about this, doesn't it? But this is merely a learned response, a knee-jerk reaction. It also seems logical, at some level, to quit your job when you fall into a really low mood. Why? Because when you're feeling bad, life seems hopeless and difficult. Your future looks uncertain, even bleak. But despite the way it looks, you usually don't quit your job because you know things will probably look a whole lot better tomorrow.

When you think in a negative manner, you're actually practicing being unhappy.

Learning to be more optimistic means examining the way you relate to your thinking. Do you feel compelled to follow each negative train of thought that enters your mind as if you have been mandated to do so? Or do you have the perspective that thoughts will come and go and you don't have to pay attention to the ones that interfere with the quality of your life? Do you see your thoughts as merely thoughts, or do you engage them, focus on them, perceive them as important, and allow them to disturb you?

How Victoria Changed Her Attitude

My client Victoria was entangled in the web of negative thinking. She saw the dark side of virtually everything. If the weather was cold, she called it gloomy. An optimist might think of cold weather as invigorating. If the weather was warm, she pronounced it muggy. An optimist might think of it as balmy. If she was trying to merge into traffic and after two cars passed someone politely allowed her into the lane, she would think, "Those two other drivers were jerks." An optimist would think she was lucky to be let into the flow of traffic.

At first, like many pessimists, Victoria didn't see herself as needing a more positive attitude. She believed that "life was all screwed up." The only way she would ever feel better was to have everyone change to her satisfaction. Obviously this wasn't going to happen. However, her previous therapist acted as if it were possible. She encouraged Victoria to "work on her anger" (I still have trouble understanding what therapists mean by this) and express her negative feelings. Victoria got really good at that, so good, in fact, that she could actually see imperfections in the beautiful flowers outside my office window.

The shift in Victoria's attitude came as she began to under-stand the role her thinking played in the way she felt. She needed to be convinced that there was a direct, point-to-point relationship between thinking negative and feeling negative. I had her do an unusual experiment that I have since used on hundreds of people. I asked her to come up with a strategy to achieve the goal of feeling as angry as possible. She immedi-ately got the point when she realized that the only way to make herself angry was to think about something that made her angry.

As Victoria gradually became convinced that it was her thinking about life, not life itself, that represented the prob-lem in the way she felt, she was able to begin making a shift. She realized that she had been fighting an uphill battle—she had been trying to make the world conform to her wishes, a battle she could not win.

Often the simple realization that you are in charge of and able to change your own attitude can be a very liberating in-sight, as was true with Victoria. Rather than spending your time and energy trying to get the world to change, you can spend that same energy looking for what's right. And when you do, you feel a whole lot better.

Optimism Makes Life More Fun

Part of the process of becoming more optimistic, of cultivating a more positive attitude, is to see clearly what's in it for you. That's easy to define: more happiness and productivity, less defensiveness, and a better experience of life on the whole.

First, you will experience more happiness because the way you feel is so closely linked to the thoughts you pay attention to. As you put less energy into negativity and dismiss more of your negative thoughts, you keep your attention (for the most part) on what's right with your life. To put it succinctly, optimists feel better than pessimists.

Second, when you become more optimistic, your productivity greatly increases because you expend less energy being caught up in your thinking. Rather than being consumed and distracted by your negativity, you can put your attention more on the task at hand—you become more oriented to the present. In this way, you can learn to be a more effective, energetic person.

> *The life of an optimist is making the best out of any situation. Becoming an optimist will improve the overall quality of your life.*

Third, by developing a more positive attitude you become less defensive. Optimists tend to see the bigger picture. Life to an optimist isn't all about himself or herself; it's about seeing the beauty in life and the possibilities at hand. To a pessimist, life seems to be all about himself or herself; it's about how life and its many challenges affect him or her. When a new housing development is being planned in the neighborhood, for example, a pessimistic man ponders its effect on him—there's going to be more noise, traffic, and perhaps crime. He thinks through the negative consequences—the people moving in might have noisy dogs, pesky children, poor taste in housepaint colors. Because he thinks so much about himself and how events and circumstances relate to him, a pessimist, over the long haul, tends to feel threatened by anything or anyone that rocks his boat. He becomes defensive to protect his self-interest against perceived threats. When someone questions his attitude, he'll point to all that's wrong with his life to support his beliefs. The more he's questioned, the more fixated he becomes.

By becoming more optimistic in your outlook, you can greatly reduce the tendency to feel threatened and therefore defensive. Because you'll be looking for what's right rather than what's wrong, you'll see that there really isn't anything to feel threatened by. In the example of the new housing development, here's how a more positive attitude might help. Suppose your neighbor approaches you and says, "You know, this new development is going to be very nice. Our homes might not look so good in comparison. What are you going to do?" If you're a pessimist, you might say in a defensive tone, "My house was here first and it looks just fine. Leave me alone." The internal assumption is made that you are in some way being attacked, and that the appropriate response is to fight back. Even if your neighbor were to insist that he didn't mean anything by his comment, you'd probably believe that he had hidden motives, possibly unknown even to him.

If you're an optimist, however, this same scenario looks different. When your neighbor says to you, "Our homes might not look so good in comparison," you say in a hopeful tone, "You know, you're probably right. If all of us can improve the appearance of our homes, even cosmetically, we might be able to improve their value quite substantially." An optimist believes in the inherent good in people—he doesn't assume he is being attacked. Even if he is attacked, he tends to make allowances for the fact that people are less than perfect and that sometimes we all say and do things that aren't as kind as we'd like.

An optimistic outlook is a hopeful one. It allows you to see the good in others and in life. It encourages you to be your best because strength and improvement usually give rise to more strength. In other words, if you're good at something— writing, for example, or tennis, or reading—the fact that you recognize your skill encourages you to feel good about yourself, which makes you eager to sharpen your skills even more. Your success feeds on itself and becomes a way of life.

Being a Pessimist Isn't Easy

A pessimist has a more difficult time because practically everything is seen as a burden—her job, her family, her chores and responsibilities. Everything is looked at in terms of how difficult it is—or how someone else doesn't have to do it. Even washing dishes is seen as a real chore. Instead of going to work and finding something wonderful about it, she spends the day wishing she were home. But once she gets home she discovers that home isn't that great either.

> *A pessimist keeps postponing his enjoyment because his thoughts are always directed toward the ways that life could be better than it is.*

It's an endless negative loop, a monster that is absolutely insatiable. Even if life does get better, a pessimist will see something else that needs to improve.

It doesn't serve you to be a pessimist! A pessimistic attitude works against you, robbing you of joy and satisfaction. On the other hand, becoming an optimist will greatly improve the quality of your life. The difference between the two is only a state of mind—a way of looking at things. With a little work, you can transform your attitude and become a true optimist.

Is an Optimist a Pollyanna?

> *An optimist believes in himself and in his ability to
> effect positive change.*

I have discussed optimism in my private work with clients
and in front of audiences for more than a decade and have
been confronted repeatedly by the same objection. I call this
objection the fear of becoming a Pollyanna.

Pollyanna, of course, was the sweet young heroine who always saw the bright side of a given situation—so much so that
she was seen (by pessimists, of course) to be unrealistic and
blinded by her optimism.

For some reason, many pessimists believe that turning to
optimism is tantamount to blinding themselves to the facts of
life, becoming apathetic, and setting themselves up to be
walked on. Let me address each of these three erroneous
concerns.

An optimist doesn't pretend that things are other than they
are—he or she accepts things as they are. There is an enormous, important difference between the two. Let's compare
the reactions of two clients, Fred, an optimist, and Gene, a
pessimist, when both lose their jobs at the same plant.

Fred, an optimist, refuses to feel hopeless and defeated and
won't entertain pessimistic thoughts about not being able to
find another job. He tells himself, and actually believes, that
everything will work out okay. He knows he didn't lose his job
on purpose. He works on the assumption that this probably
means he will find an even better job.

Gene, a pessimist, feels defeated, immobilized, and angry.
He feels sorry for himself, as if he were a victim. He tells himself that he most likely won't be able to find another job because the economy is so bad. He complains to his friends and
decides to go have a drink at the bar.

The question is, who's being realistic and who's burying his head in the sand? From my way of seeing life, Fred is in touch with reality, while Gene is completely out to lunch. Fred's focus is on the possibilities. He doesn't know for sure what's going to happen, so he chooses to assume that he will find another job. He sees this as realistic thinking, in part because he's good at what he does and in part because he has been employed for ten straight years. History shows him that he's employable.

Gene, on the other hand, is putting his attention on his negative thoughts about what might happen. Even though the evidence suggests otherwise (i.e., he is also good at his job and has been gainfully employed at the same job as Fred), he disregards the facts and points to the negative possibilities.

Who's right? It's too early to tell for sure, but Fred is lengthening the odds in his favor, while Gene is wasting his time and energy. A pessimist would surely believe that Fred is being unrealistic and too optimistic, and would point to statistics on the number of people unemployed to prove his position. An optimist knows his actions are preceded by his thoughts. To an optimist, negative thinking is similar to shooting himself in the foot.

The second major objection to optimism—that it makes you apathetic—is also grounded in ignorance. An optimist believes in herself and in her ability to effect positive change. She believes that if she does her best, there's nothing she can't do. If an optimist loses her job, she may work night and day finding a new one. If she fails, she will believe that she simply hasn't looked in the right places, and that eventually she will be successful. If an optimist faces a life-threatening illness, she will believe that it's always possible to recover and that if anyone can do it, she most certainly will be the one. This positive attitude leads to positive, productive action.

The notion that optimists are apathetic stems from pessimists who observe optimists after a failure. An optimist rarely sulks or complains after a failure. Instead, he believes that everything will work out just fine. A pessimist, because after a failure or disappointment he usually believes his world is falling hopelessly apart, mistakenly sees the optimist as apathetic. A pessimist simply can't understand how an optimist operates, so he calls it unrealistic. But it isn't.

Finally, many pessimists believe that if they were to become more optimistic, they would be sending a signal that it's okay for others to walk all over them. Again, the facts suggest otherwise. Optimists can be tremendously self-protective because they're so certain of the ultimate good and they believe so strongly in themselves. A pessimist might believe that if you give someone an inch he'll take a mile. Therefore, pessimists usually don't give an inch (or even a half inch). The result of this lack of giving is that people around them tend to feel resentful and actually try to get as much as they can from them—or go away completely—therefore validating the pessimist's viewpoint.

An optimist, on the other hand, goes ahead and gives an inch (or two), knowing that most people *don't* take advantage of others. The recipients of this giving attitude feel comfortable with the optimistic viewpoint and most of the time respond gratefully and not greedily. So the optimist ends up validating his position as well.

The difference between the optimist and the pessimist has to do with the spirit in which each operates.

On those rare occasions when someone does take advantage of an optimist, the optimist responds with appropriate action. He knows that it is sometimes in the recipient's best interest to reap the consequences of his actions. Even though an optimist may need to fire or discipline someone, or take some other form of drastic action, he does so knowing that this is ultimately in the best interests of everyone involved.

Because a pessimist tends to see everything negatively, he can't see that to an optimist firing someone from a job, disciplining a child, or taking some other seemingly harsh action can be a very positive thing to do.

It is inconceivable to me that an optimist would allow himself to be walked on, because an optimist believes that people don't deserve to be walked on. An optimist has too much self-respect to allow this to happen. A pessimist is far more likely to be walked on because he is more apt to believe that people are trying to take advantage of him.

> *To an optimist, a failure isn't the end of his world—it's a new beginning.*

The major objections to optimism can be overcome by understanding that their source is flawed. A pessimist will always believe that an optimist is unrealistic. The trick to becoming more optimistic yourself is to see the innocence in pessimism. A pessimist doesn't become one on purpose; he isn't intentionally harming himself with his attitude. He merely pays attention to his negative thinking, believes and assumes he is correct.

Many people believe that pessimists are more passionate about issues than optimists and therefore more effective—that pessimists tend to fight for what they believe in, whereas optimists tend to roll over and succumb to the tides of fate because they really don't care what happens to them. After all, they are unrealistically happy. Nonsense. When considering an issue such as a new housing development, for example, an optimist may fight even harder than the pessimist to prevent the housing development from being built. He will do whatever is possible to maintain his perceived best interest. He may attend public hearings and planning commission meetings; he may circulate petitions, organize public protests. He'll do his very best.

What he won't do is sulk if his efforts are unsuccessful. He won't feel defeated if he loses, but will begin to open to the outcome and make the experience another in a lifelong series of good experiences. Not only will he "make the best of it" (a somewhat pessimistic phrase that implies that the situation is actually negative), but he will strive to enjoy it. He thinks of the new friends and neighbors he is likely to meet, the possibility of new public services due to the increased traffic, and the likelihood that his property will increase in value. If it turns out that his property decreases in value, that's okay too. Perhaps this means he will remain in his home longer rather than relocating in a few years as he had previously thought he would. Whatever happens, in the eyes of an optimist, happens for his ultimate good—because that's what he's looking for.

The pessimist may indeed feel angry that the housing development is going to be built, but he's so busy thinking about all the negative consequences for him that he will feel too overwhelmed to do anything about it. Rather than attend public hearings and voice his legitimate objections, the pessimist will complain to his neighbors and commiserate with fellow pessimists. Rather than visit a planning commission meeting, he will say, "It never does any good anyway because no one listens and it's all political." He makes up all kinds of excuses to feel victimized and rationalizes why feeling this way is a good idea. In doing so, he reassures himself that his pessimism is more than justified.

Is a Pessimist Merely a Realist?

Recently I was asked to work with a couple on live television. The husband was an optimist and the wife a pessimist. My job was to give the pessimist advice on how she could become more optimistic—and to give the optimist advice on how to help her along. It became obvious after spending a few moments with her that she didn't see herself as a pessimist. She was convinced, as many pessimists are, that she was a realist, that her beliefs and feelings were grounded in facts, honesty, and realistic expectations. Her husband claimed that whenever anyone tried to persuade her that life wasn't really as bad as she perceived it to be, she would very cleverly, and with incredible confidence, offer evidence to support her pessimism. If someone pointed out that magnificent acts of kindness were often performed, she would counter with stories of hatred and bitterness. Her husband went so far as to say that if she were to win a five-million-dollar lottery, she would be upset because last month's winner had won ten million.

This particular pessimist is typical of thousands of others. Pessimists seldom see themselves as such, but are convinced beyond any doubt that their feelings about life are justified. I've even heard pessimists claim, "I'm not a pessimist. In fact, given how awful the world really is, I'm an optimist."

The first thing you learn if you deal with pessimists regularly, as I do, is that you can't argue with them about whether or not they're pessimistic. If you do, you'll lose—and you might even end up feeling a little pessimistic yourself. Remember, a pessimist believes that his or her way of seeing life is realistic and accurate. When questioned, the pessimist's husband confessed that he had spent most of his married life trying to convince his wife of her pessimism and her inaccurate way of looking at life. This, of course, only convinced the wife further that people were, deep down, aggressive and negative. After all, she said, "Even my husband doesn't like me just the way I am."

A far more effective way of working with pessimists is to teach them (gently) that realism is in the eyes of the beholder—that their way of seeing life isn't wrong, but it does work against them. You need to prove to a pessimist that optimism isn't unrealistic but a legitimate way to move through life. The trick in working with this woman, as with many other pessimists, was to demonstrate that there was something of real value to be gained if she became more optimistic. She had to believe that optimism isn't a pretense that life is better than it is, but that optimism is well founded. I told her a few stories that demonstrate how optimistic thinking leads to successful results.

> *True optimism isn't contingent upon eventual success.*

One story in particular has helped many pessimists open their eyes to optimism. An acquaintance of mine was in search of his "ideal career." He had an idea for a home-based business unlike any he had ever heard of, having to do with commercial software designed to simplify a few standard programs. Being an optimist, he pursued his dream, and like most people in pursuit of their dreams, he ran into a little resistance and a few minor hurdles. It was almost funny to listen to him explain resistance from others because his optimism shined through so brightly. He spoke to about a hundred people in similar lines of work, and every one insisted that his idea would fail. Rather than get discouraged, he assumed that he was speaking to the wrong people, and that in time someone would be able to help him. Sure enough, a month or two later he ran into the perfect person who was able to "see" his idea and offer him the advice he sought. Today his business is extremely successful and my friend the optimist is very happy.

The most refreshing part of his story, even more than his business success, was the way this optimist reacted *after* it became apparent that his idea was going to be a smash hit in the marketplace. He didn't spend one second saying, or even thinking, "I told you so," to his friends and colleagues who'd been so sure he would fail. He insists that the people who scoffed actually helped him as much or more than the person who eventually provided the advice he needed. He claims that his critics convinced him his idea really was unique and that this help was what enabled him to persevere.

As you spend time around true optimists like this man, you begin to realize a significant point: Had this business venture proven unsuccessful in terms of the bottom line, my acquaintance would have been just as happy as he is today. Rather than attach conditions to his happiness and self-esteem, an optimist does the opposite. He feels good about himself first, and then out of his feeling of self-assurance he attempts to succeed. If this man's business venture had been a failure, my hunch is that he would have believed that this too was in his ultimate best interest. He would have learned what he could from his hard work and experiences and then done something else equally wonderful with his life.

An Optimist Knows There Are Many Truths

I have found myself thinking in a similar optimistic way when a publisher has turned down a manuscript or idea of mine. Rather than complain, feel sorry for myself, and think of all the negative implications, I assume that I have simply contacted the wrong publisher, or that I haven't yet succeeded in articulating my idea in the best way possible. In the worst case, it has happened that no matter how hard I tried, my writing simply couldn't find an appropriate home. But this is okay too. I can learn all sorts of wonderful things from my rejections—things that don't show up when I succeed.

An optimist isn't saying that there aren't negative things going on—she just knows that there are negative and positive characteristics in every situation, so she chooses to focus on the more positive ones. An optimist instinctively realizes that the quality of her thinking determines the quality of her life. If she chooses to direct her thinking toward what's right with her life, that's what she will see—and that's what she will experience. To an optimist, the quality of life is lived in her own head. There are always many ways to view a given situation and it's up to us to decide which one we will focus on.

When you're an optimist, you look for ways to succeed, for what's right in a situation, for the grain of gold in the sand. If you don't see what you're looking for, you look somewhere else. I once heard psychologist Wayne Dyer say, "Pessimists, when looking for a parking place in the crowded city, literally are looking for no place to park." What he means, of course, is that pessimists are so busy complaining about the lack of parking that all they can see are the filled spaces. Optimists, on the other hand, are looking for the perfect place to park. If they don't see a parking place, they assume that they haven't yet found the one reserved just for them.

The Fable of the Wise Man and the Villagers

There once was a very poor city of a few thousand citizens. On top of the tallest mountain near the village lived the town's wise man. Whenever someone sought guidance or wisdom, he would travel up the hill to speak with this man.

One day a large stray horse appeared on a farmer's land. Everyone in the village began celebrating the farmer's good fortune. "This is a true blessing," they insisted. "Life will be so much easier for him now." But when the villagers asked the wise man to verify their certainty, he simply said, "Maybe so, maybe not." The villagers questioned his wisdom. It seemed so obvious they were right.

A few days later, the farmer's oldest son, on whom he depended for his family's survival, was riding the horse when he fell and broke his leg. The villagers were horrified. The wise man had been right. How did he know? "This was surely the worst thing that could have possibly happened," they insisted. The villagers ran up the mountain to verify their assumption—but were shocked to hear the wise man's response. When asked if this was the worst thing that could have happened, he replied, "Maybe so, maybe not." The villagers again questioned his wisdom. It seemed so obvious they were right.

A few weeks later the army came marching through the village. War had broken out and the army had come to take all able-bodied men to die for the cause. Of course the farmer's son couldn't go; his life was spared. When the villagers ran to the wise man to praise him for seeing that everything had been for the best, all the wise man would say was, "Maybe so, maybe not."

Optimism is a choice that you can make—but so is pessimism.

The most relevant difference between an optimist and a pessimist is that a pessimist assumes the worst—and he is convinced he is right. Whatever happens, he can find what's wrong, and he can think the problems out into the future to some "logical" conclusion, which of course, will be negative. An optimist is less certain in his predictions. He admits that ultimately he doesn't really know what's going to happen, and because there are so many "truthful" ways to look at any given situation, he may as well choose the most positive direction to focus on.

If you admit the truth, that life is impossible to predict with absolute certainty, you'll begin to see that optimism is your best course of action.

Why Is Optimism a Shortcut Through Therapy?

Optimism is a shortcut because the best part of happiness and personal growth starts when you open your eyes to optimism. The whole point of therapy is to grow and develop, solve problems, and become more contented. When you discover optimism these goals become more visible. You can look at your childhood with curiosity, your present circumstances with openness and clarity, and your future with hope and vision.

Pessimism keeps you trapped in negativity. When you look at your past through pessimistic eyes you see a difficult childhood. You tend to blame your past, your parents, your upbringing, for the way you are today. Rather than learning quickly from your past and moving on, you tend to dwell on what was wrong and wish it had been different. When you look at your past optimistically, you'll see it in terms of the valuable lessons you can learn from it. Through pessimistic eyes you see your past as a series of hardships that must be struggled with and overcome.

> **Optimism breeds growth.**

Problems, when looked at optimistically, are seen as challenges. When looked at pessimistically, the same problems are seen as tremendous battles to be fought. To an optimist, relationships are opportunities to connect with partners in life; the goal is to see the beauty and love in others. The differences among people, to an optimist, are more evidence that relationships are interesting and wonderful.

To a pessimist, relationships are seen as needing to be worked on. One goal is to change others, or oneself, in order to cope with our incredible differences. To a pessimist, relationships are inherently difficult and problems are inevitable.

Being caught up in her thinking, to a pessimist, means it's time to roll up her sleeves and get to work on her life. It's time to analyze what's wrong, "get to the bottom of all this important stuff," and so on.

Being caught up in her thinking, to an optimist, simply means she is caught up. Somehow, she assumes, she has strayed from her path; she isn't seeing things as clearly as she can. Perhaps it's time to take a step back and gain some perspective.

To a pessimist, it will look as if an optimist is caught up in denial, that she isn't looking at her life in an honest way—that if she were to look closer, be more honest, she would see how terrible her life really was. But this isn't true.

When you aren't caught up in your thinking, when your mind is free from an overabundance of distraction, you have the ability to see your life clearly. When you aren't bothered by the little things, when you have perspective, when you can make allowances for the imperfections in yourself and in others, you become free to make the necessary adjustments in life, to grow and change. When you're pessimistic, making changes is very difficult. You may see many problems, but the solutions will often remain invisible.

This is why I see optimism as a prerequisite to personal growth. When you look for ways to learn from your experiences—rather than focusing exclusively on everything that's wrong with your life—you keep the doors wide open for new and exciting discoveries. Whatever your goals in therapy may be, an optimistic outlook will assist you in achieving them quickly and painlessly.

PRINCIPLE FIVE:
Don't Expect Others to Think Like You

The choice of a point of view is the initial act of a culture.

—JOSÉ ORTEGA Y GASSET

In therapy, as in everyday life, one of the major concerns and topics of discussion is the way we relate (or don't relate) to others. How often do you find yourself saying things like "Why did she say that?", "I would never do it that way," or "It makes me so angry when he does that." Isn't it true that a great deal of our frustration in life has to do with our lack of understanding as to why other people behave or react the way they do? Don't we spend too much time disapproving of the actions and attitudes of others? Don't we wish other people were more like us? How many people have genuinely come to peace with the fact that literally no one behaves, lives, or reacts to life the way they do?

On a superficial level, most of us come to an eventual understanding that all people are unique. If I asked one hundred people the question "Are you unique?" most would answer in the affirmative. Unfortunately, almost no one uses this understanding as the vehicle for releasing himself or herself from frustration about others. Instead, most people continue pointing to individual differences and blaming these differences for their troubles. In this chapter I will show you how to view your differences in a new light, enabling you to enjoy and flow with, rather than struggle against, your differences from others.

Often a major goal in therapy is to understand the far-reaching implications of the fact that we are all different—and to come to peace with this understanding. Without this acceptance, a person will spend much of life frustrated because very few people will meet his or her expectations over the long term. Each of us will meet and have relationships with people who behave in ways that seem foreign to us or confuse us.

There are two ways to go about understanding our differences from other people. The first way, which is often the approach used in long-term therapy, is to focus on each *specific difference* you're concerned with. If you believe it's important to expose your children to classical music and fine art and your spouse doesn't, you could easily spend a great deal of time discussing this difference. But while it's true that *some* discussion might be useful, there is a tendency on the part of many therapists to go overboard, to hook you in to the specific details instead of focusing on the broader, deeper principle involved. Understanding the principle (we all see things differently), not the specific details (whether it's right or wrong to expose your children to fine art and music), is ultimately what allows you to move beyond frustration to a state of mind in which compromise, compassion for other points of view, and personal growth are possible. A therapy session that focused on the fact that our differences are okay would be a therapy session well spent.

But instead of this broader approach, here's how it typically works: If you're in marriage counseling, your therapist may refer to the specific difference (classical music) dozens or even hundreds of times, encouraging you to talk through your differences or work on your communication skills. The problem with this approach is that there is no end to it. You could spend your entire hourlong session discussing this issue every week for six months and it would get you nowhere—except back to your therapist's office. There will always be new angles to discuss, validity to each point of view, and new frustrations. Pretty soon you can start to believe that the important issue isn't the scope of your differences but the specific issue of classical music. Once you believe this, you'll have a strong tendency to focus on other specific differences until, at some point, every difference you have with your spouse (and there will be many) will start to irritate you. Your focus will then start to be on those differences instead of the love you have for each other.

To continually discuss your differences, regardless of what a specific difference happens to be, or how relevant it seems to be, will only ensure that *you* will feel the effects of these thoughts, which will invariably be negative. And once you're feeling negative, you're going to be even more inclined to blame your differences for the way you're feeling. It's an endless negative cycle that is very difficult to break. The cycle certainly won't be broken by even more discussion.

What's more, as you learned when we discussed moods, *every single time* you fall into another low mood, this issue or any issue is going to seem very important and you'll be tempted to believe the issue must be dealt with at that moment. Regardless of how much time you spend discussing the issue, each low mood you experience will bring it back as if it never left.

The way out of this negative loop isn't to focus on each specific difference you have with others, but to realize that differences are a necessary part of life and to learn to expect, appreciate, and make allowances for them.

What should your therapist do? Instead of focusing on and referring constantly to any specific difference, your therapist would be doing you an enormous favor if he or she could teach you why you have differences, and where they come from. This is a step beyond merely discussing why the specific issue of music or art is bothering you. This deeper knowledge would show you how to accept and enjoy rather than be troubled by your differences. Instead of being concerned by the fact that you view something differently than another, you would instead view it as natural, saying to yourself, "Of course I see this differently." As new differences revealed themselves in your life, assuming you had gained the necessary added perspective, you would be equipped to deal with them— whatever they happened to be—instead of having to return to your therapist to discuss the new issue.

Your goal should be to understand that *all* differences are predictable and that all viewpoints are innocently formed. We developed many of our opinions and beliefs early on by listening and learning from the significant people in our lives. As we internalized certain messages about life—the way things are, our strengths and weaknesses, and so on, we had no way of knowing whether the information we were accepting as "truth" was going to serve us in our eventual quest for a happy life or was going to bring us hardship and pain. We were innocent onlookers—but now we have the capacity to change. Understanding this enables you to let go of your need to analyze each specific incident as it arises in your relationships and your need to defend your positions. Can you imagine how much more peaceful your life would be if your disagreements with others genuinely didn't bother you?

> *No one else is like you. This truth is one of the most liberating principles you can ever master.*

To help you move through therapy quickly and effectively, it should be the therapist's job to teach you to become peaceful about differences, an important part of life that doesn't have to frustrate you. When you feel unperturbed about differences in general, it becomes much easier to discuss any specific differences you do have. Most people do the opposite. They attempt to focus on the discord so that a more desirable feeling can surface between two or more people (which rarely happens) or so that common ground can be found. The far more effective and direct route is to first regain a more peaceful feeling within yourself through understanding the nature and innocence of differences, making them seem less significant and easier to discuss. This is precisely what I attempt to do when I'm hired as a mediator between two or more people who believe they absolutely can't see eye to eye. I teach them that this need not be their goal. Instead, their goal must be to know that it's not important to see eye to eye.

A person who is concerned about the fact that he has a difference of opinion with someone about a particular issue will likely use that issue as ammunition to keep himself unhappy. He'll think about the issue, talk about it, focus on it, only because he hasn't come to grips with the deeper notion of differences. The fact that he continues to be bothered or annoyed keeps him from seeing even a grain of truth in other points of view.

When examined in a positive, loving way, your differences with others can be appreciated for what they can contribute to your life. Compromise is effortless and growth is possible. Those same dissimilarities, when examined with a negative, pessimistic attitude, are irritating and bothersome. Compromise is usually impossible and growth is difficult.

Think of a good friend. Are the two of you identical? Do you have the same views on everything? Doubtful. The truth is, many good friends, even "best friends," have surprisingly little in common—or at least they have plenty of significant differences. What they do share is a warm feeling of love and rapport. This feeling of rapport makes the differences they have seem insignificant.

When put into proper perspective and understood fully, differences can bring you joy rather than pain.

Think of someone you don't particularly care for. Even if she is different from you the way your best friend is different from you, your feeling toward those differences is quite different. For example, you may love to exercise, while your best friend doesn't. Because she's your friend, you've learned to overlook this difference—it's a nonissue. You might, however, dislike someone else and use her lack of interest in exercise as one of your reasons. Obviously, the incompatibilities themselves aren't the problem.

> *One of the greatest gifts a therapist can offer you is a sense of perspective about the great variety of human beings.*

To fully appreciate our differences we need to understand their roots—why we're all unique and why this *has* to be. We need to become convinced of the perfect innocence that makes up our differences. Once you are convinced of this, you'll cease to become frustrated simply because someone is behaving in a way you don't agree with.

Why We All Must Be Unique

My wife and I traveled to India a few years ago and were impressed with the incredible differences between the Indian and American cultures. I remember a funny incident shortly after we arrived. We were in a large group of people and I began to feel a bit claustrophobic. It seemed almost as though the people nearest to me were intentionally crowding me. I remember feeling irritated and a little self-righteous, thinking, "I would never crowd someone like that." That evening I shared my experience with another American. Chuckling, he informed me that I was simply experiencing part of Indian culture. It turns out that our idea of "personal space" is just that, personal. It's ours. As a culture, we made up a silent rule that we will stand a certain distance from the other person nearest to us whenever possible—and we will consider this common courtesy. The Indian culture has a different rule about personal space—the Indian idea of a polite distance might be half that of ours, or less. Neither culture questions this implicit rule. Nor is either culture right or wrong.

A magical transformation took place inside me the moment I understood what was happening. Rather than feeling irritated and self-righteous, I became interested in the cultural difference.

You've probably experienced similar differences between yourself and individuals from other cultures. Perhaps you know that many Mexican citizens take a *siesta* in the middle of the day when you and I might be working. Or maybe you've heard that in many European countries, people drink coffee well into the night when you and I might be sleeping.

The principle of separate realities says that the differences between individuals from the same culture are every bit as vast as those of different cultures. For some reason, however, we have learned to respect and anticipate cultural differences in other nations, yet resist and even resent the natural differences among people in our culture. I remember hearing a story about President Clinton. Allegedly, he carefully studied a pamphlet detailing some of our major cultural differences on his plane trip to South Korea so that he wouldn't offend anyone. Yet that very evening he became irritated at someone in his cabinet for disagreeing with him. It never occurred to the president (or his cabinet member) that the two of them were also living in separate "cultures." This same phenomenon happens to most of us many times a day. We tend to lack the appropriate understanding and appreciation of our differences, especially on a personal level, which causes us unnecessary, continuing pain.

Your Thought System Is Unique

Each of us has what is called a thought system, a psychological filter that information passes through before it gets to our awareness, through which we see the world. Our thought system is like a pair of sunglasses that we keep on all the time. It is a complex, interwoven pattern of thoughts, linked into opinions, beliefs, and expectations. It is our thought system that enables us to compare new facts or experiences with what has come before.

Although your thought system serves you well by allowing you to make comparisons and judgments, it's critical to know that your thought system contains all the information you've accumulated over your lifetime. By necessity, then, it's always *past* information your thought system uses to distinguish right from wrong, important from unimportant, and so on. Your thought system thus is your source of conditioned thought. In other words, when you rely on it, you're thinking in a habitual way, in a sense programmed to react in a certain manner.

To fully appreciate how powerful thought systems are, you must realize that they are absolutely self-validating. In other words, your thinking will convince you that you are seeing things accurately. For example, if your thought system includes the idea that no one cares about other people anymore, the following scenario becomes possible. You pick up the morning paper and notice that on page thirteen there is an article about the return of skinhead gangs. You chuckle, because in your mind you have been proved right once again. You call up a friend who has a more positive outlook about people and tell him about the article. "You see, what have I been telling you all these years? More and more people are turning evil." Little do you know that a feature article in that same paper discusses the return of volunteerism in America. Such is the nature of thought systems. We're constantly seeking validation of what we already believe.

> *Our thought system is a self-contained unit through which we see the world—like a pair of sunglasses that we never take off.*

Because our thought systems are filled with our memories of the past, they encourage us to continue to see things as we have before. This is why most of us have a strong tendency to react negatively (or positively) to similar situations repeatedly throughout our lifetimes. Very simply, we're interpreting our present circumstances in the same way we have before. A woman who believes that men can't be trusted will look for verification of this belief each time she's with a man, whether or not the man is trustworthy. More often than not, she'll do this without conscious awareness.

Because each thought system is unique, it's impossible for two people, from the same culture or not, to view life in precisely the same manner. There is no way you're going to see life as someone else does. There are absolutely no exceptions to this rule.

For example, two clients of mine, Tom and Marie, who were married after knowing each other only a very short while, have differing viewpoints regarding what is important when he or she isn't feeling well. When Tom isn't feeling well, he likes to be left entirely alone. He doesn't want any attention, especially from Marie. He doesn't want breakfast in bed, flowers delivered to his room, or even a morning newspaper. He wants to be left alone period. Tom's perception is that if Marie truly loves him, she will respect his wishes completely.

Unfortunately, Marie looks at not feeling well in just the opposite way. She wants to be pampered. She feels that she needs others' sympathy, especially Tom's—and that if he truly loves her, he will go out of his way to exhibit kindness and caring.

The first time Marie was ill, Tom did (in his own way), exhibit enormous concern—he left the house for about twelve hours! Marie, of course, was crushed. She immediately felt that Tom didn't care. In fact, just the opposite was true: Tom felt that he was doing Marie a big favor by leaving. After all, he told himself, who would want to be bothered by someone else when she wasn't feeling well?

Unfortunately, many human conflicts are not as humorous as this one. Many of us take our own preferences very seriously in far more important areas—the "right" way to raise a child, the "proper" way to spend money, and so forth. The important lesson is to understand that all human differences can be less threatening to us when we understand their source.

Humility Brings Harmony

The humility that comes from an understanding of separate realities is genuine and instantly helpful in terms of fostering your relationships with other people. Humility allows you to see that your own ideas about life cannot be superior to anyone else's. The information contained in your thought system (and mine) is every bit as arbitrary as the next person's.

Make Allowances for Others

> *There's no getting around the fact that each of us, to one degree or another, is controlled by our own thought system.*

When we realize that all of us *arbitrarily* develop our existing beliefs as if they were absolute reality, we can quickly let go of our need to be right. We all know how difficult it can be to change our minds about something we feel strongly about, and this is what all of us are up against many times a day. Each time you disagree with someone, that person is equally convinced that he or she is correct and *you* are the one who isn't seeing or interpreting the facts correctly. The beliefs and conclusions expressed by your counterpart are a result of his or her past experiences. So are yours. The fact that the two of you disagree is predictable. It couldn't be any other way.

"Even if what you say is true," you might think to yourself, "my view of life is a good one and I don't want to change." The point here isn't to change your thought system, but to see its arbitrary nature. It's not that your thought system is wrong, but that it was developed through your own unique set of circumstances and through your own form of thinking. You don't need to tamper with the contents of your thought system to begin to feel better, but you do need to begin to accept the fact that everyone's got his or her own unique thought system.

I heard a song on the radio that had, as its basic message, "What's the use of staying together if you don't see eye to eye?" This is a common belief that causes a great deal of unnecessary hardship. The truth is, you can't see eye to eye with anyone all the time. You could spend the rest of your life attempting to find someone who shares your every dream and attitude, but you'd end up disappointed. As you get to know people, you discover that thought systems were formed individually and won't merge simply because you want them to.

The fact that you're married to someone, or work closely with someone, does *not* make it more likely that the two of you will see eye to eye. In fact, just the opposite is probable. The more time you spend with someone, the more chances there are for your separate realities to surface. Despite this, many of us tend to expect (or secretly want) those closest to us to conform to the way we think about life. This is not only unfair, it's unrealistic.

A thought system is the mechanism that convinces us that our own version of life is accurate.

We honestly believe that we see "truth." We feel our feelings and believe that others share those feelings—and if they don't, we believe there's something wrong with them. We believe that our opinions, beliefs, prejudices, even certainties, are grounded in truth. We find ourselves thinking, "Why can't he understand me?"

Thus the practical implications of the knowledge that we all see life so differently is powerful. When you *expect* to see things differently and take it as a foregone conclusion that everyone will react differently than you will to the identical stimulus, you can begin to make allowances for other people's behavior and reactions and virtually eliminate quarrels between yourself and others. These allowances are a signal that you've gained a sense of perspective.

You don't have to see eye to eye with someone in order to love and respect him or her. All you need is the knowledge that you can't see eye to eye. This understanding allows you to find any common ground and to build on it. In instances where there isn't any common ground, it allows you to listen to other points of view with respect and interest. Once you understand that no one will ever see life as you do, and you come to peace with this understanding, you'll stop expending energy in attempting to change others. You'll be free to enjoy and learn from your differences with others.

So often we have as a silent goal getting others to come around to our way of seeing things. This goal encourages us to feel and act defensively toward other points of view and discourages us from listening. But once you realize that this goal isn't feasible, and isn't necessary, you can see differences in a whole new way.

Let me share with you a personal story about a situation in which my wife and I were helped by an understanding of separate realities. What seems like a long time ago, right before our first child was born, we were talking about taking a trip as a last chance to get away before the joys of parenting began. In my mind, I was planning a romantic getaway—music, private time, walks on the beach. We agreed that this time I would choose the place. When I approached my wife with my decision to travel to the Northwest, her eyes lit up like a Christmas tree. Her initial response to my suggestion was "The Northwest, great! We can spend the week with my parents!"

This story is funny to me because I have worked with so many clients over the years who have become frustrated over a similar situation. "Why can't my husband or wife have the same thoughts about life and the same priorities as I do?"

To my wife and me, however, this was a typical example of two people viewing something in a different way—to be expected. I tend to romanticize vacations and my wife has a deep and committed love of family.

> **What could be nicer than two individuals who love each other, yet appreciate the fact that differences in psychological wiring are a fact of life?**

Most clients, when they hear stories such as this one, begin to understand the innocence in our own preferences—and the preferences of others. After all, we don't develop our preferences intentionally and we certainly don't develop them to hurt or offend others. Instead, preferences, beliefs, attitudes, reactions, and opinions are developed through the silent, habitual process of filtering stored information through our own thought system.

Once you discover the reason behind differences, (that is, separate realities), you'll develop a healthy humility regarding your own thought system. You'll see that your thought system, too, was created by our own thoughts and would have been very different had the input been different. You and the people you disagree with most could quite easily have been the best of friends had your experiences been different. This new humility that comes from understanding makes it very difficult to be angry or frustrated at someone simply because he or she sees life differently than you do.

You can tell whether you're properly incorporating the principle of separate realities into your life by determining whether or not you feel irritated at someone. If you do, even a little bit, then in all likelihood you're missing some element of the principle. When you *expect* people to react to you in ways that you don't understand, you'll find that the level of compassion you have for yourself and for others rises instantly and dramatically. When we let go of our expectations of others, we allow ourselves to engage fully with the person we are with without the contamination of our own thought systems. Frustration diminishes, and we maximize the potential of the relationship.

Don't Take Anything Personally

The principle of separate realities isn't merely a theory to read about and then toss aside. When you understand the *fact* of separate realities you'll see that there is no logical reason to take personally what others say and do.

Most of us spend our entire lifetime formulating our personal version of life and then attempting to prove that it's accurate and valid. The views we formulate originate within ourselves and nowhere else. You personally have nothing whatsoever to do with the thoughts that I formulate about you. Had I been programmed differently, I would have had a different response. If I'm programmed to be irritated when someone is late, this is my programming, not yours. If you walk in late to see me, guess what? I'm likely to be irritated. But the irritation stems from inside me. And if you know this is the case, why should you be offended by my reaction? You won't be.

This understanding helps many couples in my stress management practice. As individuals begin to see how all opinions and reactions are formed, where they come from, and how predictable they really are, they begin to soften and make allowances in their own reactions to others. Whether the differences have to do with finances, child-rearing, sex, approaches to work, or any other typical area of contention, this simple understanding of separate realities plays a major role in easing the tension.

Become an Anthropologist

> *Become genuinely interested in the way other people see life and how they react to various circumstances.*

In many ways, what I am suggesting is that you become an anthropologist, of sorts, a student of human behavior. Begin studying people.

Instead of being annoyed because someone isn't like you, consider the curiosity or fascination of that person. Instead of saying, "I can't believe he acts like that," say to yourself, "Oh, that's how he sees it in his world."

Don't do this, however, while deep down you are still feeling annoyed. Don't try to trick yourself. Instead, take a hard and honest look at what's being said here. Strive to understand that every human being is wired very differently and there were many factors that went into our programming: our parents, our siblings, our upbringing, our positive experiences and our negative experiences. The frustration with others arises when we either "expect" others to see life as we do or think they "should" see life as we do. Neither is true. If you want to move beyond frustration, come to see that people can't see life the way you do—and they never will.

Your Psychological Defenses Will Fade Away

One of the important personal growth concepts you're likely to learn about in therapy is that of defense mechanisms. In a nutshell, a defense mechanism is a psychological tool we use to protect ourselves from consciously or unconsciously perceived threats. You might learn to protect yourself from rejection by turning down offers to be with other people. The unconscious motivation says, "If I'm the one who says no, then no one else can reject me." Because defense mechanisms are often self-destructive, it's in your best interest to learn the ways you sabotage yourself so that you can stop doing so.

The understanding of separate realities brings us undeniably closer to other people and assists us greatly in dropping our own defense mechanisms. It also assists us in helping others to drop their defenses, because being accepting of others shows them that it's safe to be open and accepting of us.

> *When you approach someone, not in an attempt to change or prove him or her wrong, but with a genuine interest and respect for the way he or she views life, defenses drop and hearts begin to open.*

When you understand the fact that we are all very different, not as a concept but as a fact of life, it's difficult *not* to be interested in other points of view—including those of people you may have come to believe you couldn't possibly like. Once you see the way each of us has picked up our beliefs and opinions, you begin to appreciate the differences in people. This, in turn, opens your eyes to the beauty and mystery of diversity. You begin to appreciate and respect other points of view, not because you know others will approve of your new attitude, but because you've opened to an important principle of life.

Harmony Is Based on Allowing Differences

In a piece of music, if everyone sings the same note, there is no harmony at all. Only by allowing different melodies to sound at the same time do we achieve the beauty of harmony.

Many people believe that it's critical to share similar, if not identical, beliefs and values with someone with whom they have a relationship. While this may seem preferable, it's far from mandatory. Individuals from extremely diverse backgrounds have learned to overlook their differences and live harmonious, loving lives together. I've seen people from opposite ends of the spectrum economically and politically that ended up in happy, lasting marriages. I've seen couples from different ethnic groups merge into harmonious relationships, and I've seen people from different religions come together for a strong, lasting bond. Furthermore, as mentioned earlier, many good friends have little in common except a warm loving feeling of respect and rapport. That's the only essential thing.

People who enjoy the best relationships with others, who live life with the least frustration regarding their differences, have learned that differences are to be expected, a fact of life. This understanding must go beyond a mere intellectual "I know we're all different." You must truly own this idea and incorporate it into your daily life.

The way I see it, we have only two realistic choices. We can resist the principle of separate realities and remain frustrated and angry over the fact that no one seems to conform to our way of thinking, or we can strive to understand what in Eastern philosophy is called "the way of things." Separate realities *is* the way things really are. Everyone is unique and has different gifts to offer. When we look for these gifts we will surely find them—and in doing so, we will open the door to a world of personal growth.

Principle Six:
Now Is the Time to Live

Life is in the here and now, not in the there and afterwards. . . . Either we meet it, we live it—or we miss it.

—Vimala Thakar

Many people postpone their inner contentment, satisfaction, and lust for life. They feel that life will be better some day, when various conditions are met. Sadly, these people invariably are the ones who live with regrets from the past and concerns over what was or what might have been.

Equally sad is the fact that many therapists actually encourage their clients to live in the past—or in the future—often without realizing they're doing so. Clients are encouraged to relive or reexperience their pasts as if doing so had some connection to happiness. They are encouraged to focus on, to think about, and, perhaps most frequently, to discuss their pasts instead of learning how to bring their attention back to the here and now. Clients are urged to "get in touch with" the negative feelings that accompany their negative thoughts of the past, even when they have declared a lack of interest in dragging up the past. Therapists, as I have mentioned, sometimes call this denial. To many therapists, denial covers virtually anything the client is unwilling to think about—even if the unwillingness has nothing to do with pretending that life is or was different than it really is or was and has everything to do with a simple preference for remaining peaceful instead of angry.

Often therapists will prompt clients to speculate about their future, causing them a great deal of worry or concern. They will inadvertently encourage their clients to get caught up in future-oriented thinking in order to "honestly assess" the future. Such attempts to help clients usually result not in a happier or more productive experience of life, or even in a helping hand toward a brighter future, but in an unhealthy dependence on the therapist. Because clients learn to regret the past and to be overly concerned with the future, and because the therapist expresses concern, comfort, and empathy, clients sometimes believe they need their therapist to "deal with" their "complex" issues.

Many people live as if their lives were a dress rehearsal for some later date.

What Is Your Therapist's Agenda?

It may sound as though I'm being too hard on therapists. Before you jump to this conclusion, let's review what therapists attempt to accomplish. To begin with, as far as I'm aware, the intentions of therapists are good. Most, if not all, are genuinely trying to help people. One major way in which therapists help is to encourage honesty, particularly with yourself. Certainly this is an admirable goal. Honesty can lead to integrity, a key component of self-esteem.

The second worthwhile goal of many therapists, closely related to honesty, is to encourage introspection, the willingness and ability to discover who you are, what you want, and what is true for you. Therapists attempt to help you distinguish between acting out of a state of fear and acting from a place of wisdom and strength. These goals and others, if achieved by a client, make therapy a useful process.

As I have attempted to make clear from the outset, my concern isn't with therapy itself but with the dependent, expensive, never-ending cycle that therapy can so often become. A significant percentage of my clients come to my office complaining of the stress they feel *as a result* of the therapy they have been in. A therapist could respond (and some have) to this by insisting that my clients are feeling stress, not because of what they learned or didn't learn in therapy, but because they are confronted with "hidden issues" that are being exposed to them in therapy. I disagree. These so-called hidden issues usually surface a year or two *after* therapy begins. It's my belief that many of these issues come about precisely because therapy has been going on so long that the client and therapist are actually looking for problems and issues. I believe that one of the hidden fears of clients in therapy is "Oh no, I'm running out of things to talk about." And one of the hidden fears of some therapists is "Oh no, we're running out of issues to discuss. What's going to happen to my practice?"

The problem with long-term therapy stems from the well-meaning yet pervasive tendency to encourage clients to move away from the present moment rather than to merge into it.

As I have already mentioned, a great deal of time in therapy is spent discussing the past as if the past were happening right now, or, alternatively, in discussing the future.

The future is nothing more than a series of present moments that will eventually arrive. And when the present moment does arrive, you must make the decision either to remain in the present or continue with the habit of speculating about future (or past) moments. The identical mental process will continue. If you fail to learn to live in the present today, or this year, it won't be any easier to learn next year. If your childhood was difficult and you're forty years old today, your childhood will still have been difficult when you're fifty years old.

I refer to this process of encouraging past- and future-oriented thinking rather than present-moment thinking as well-meaning because the therapists who encourage it believe it would be helpful. Doesn't it make sense that if you figured out why your childhood was so bad, it would help you feel better today? It seems as though it would, and indeed, perhaps a small dose of insight stemming from your past might be useful. But this past-oriented thought process will take you only so far. Eventually you must learn to live in the present moment, or you'll remain unhappy. Let me explain further.

Betty's Story—She Lived in the Past

I had a client named Betty who had given up on therapy. She came to my stress management center because she thought perhaps her problem was stress-related. Betty had spent several years discussing her childhood with a therapist. In particular, she spent a great deal of time discussing and thinking about the reasons why she couldn't maintain a positive relationship with a man. During our first visit together, Betty told me that she "absolutely knew" why she had so much trouble with men. When I asked her to explain, here is what she said: "The reason I can't get along with men is that I had a difficult relationship with my father. Whenever I get involved with someone, I think about my father, and the man inevitably reminds me of him." I responded by asking her, "How long have you known this?" Her answer: "Three years."

If knowing the reason were the critical part of the solution, shouldn't Betty have been able to have great relationships by now? She had known the reason for three years, but still was no better off than before entering therapy.

All Betty really needed to learn was the art of living more

of her life in what I call the present moment. She learned that her mind was in the habit of drifting away from where she was and from those she was with. Instead her thoughts turned backward in time to her poor relationship with her father. As she thought about her father (past-oriented thinking) she hoped her present relationship wouldn't wind up like the one she had had with him (future-oriented thinking).

Her therapist had taught Betty a few valuable points about her past in their first few sessions together. But then, rather than teach Betty a skill to help her integrate that knowledge into her life, he simply kept reviewing the same information with her in different ways for the next three years. They would discuss the specific details of Betty's relationship with her father as well as the specific ways Betty's relationships tended to fail, instead of talking about the tools she needed to keep her from repeating her mistakes. As you've already seen, discussing specific details is a never-ending process. Again, this doesn't mean it's never appropriate to discuss issues, only that it's critical that you be aware of what you're doing.

In our sessions, Betty learned that she felt cynical around men and learned to use those feelings to her advantage. Instead of comparing a man to her father, she started using her feelings as a tipoff that she was getting caught up in past- and future-oriented thinking. Once she caught herself, all she needed to do was to gently bring herself back to the present moment—reminding herself that her life was lived here and now.

A mind that isn't distracted with its own thoughts about the past or future is able to make wise, appropriate decisions.

What Should the Goals of Therapy Be?

I'm passionate about this issue because I know that present-moment thinking can help you with all aspects of your life regardless of what you happen to be going through. Your attention to the present will foster a rich, full life. Unfortunately, non-present-moment-oriented thinking can wreak havoc, even ruin your life, regardless of how positive your life might appear externally.

Whenever your mind slips away from the present, from what you're doing at any given moment, and moves forward into the future or backward to the past, two problems loom up. Unless you're reminiscing about the wonderful times you had or dreaming about an exciting, positive future, your mind will likely be regretting something that is now over or worrying about something that hasn't yet happened. In whatever direction your mind wanders, you end up the loser in terms of how you're going to feel. This being the case, it's puzzling to me (and I hope it is becoming more so for you) why so many therapists insist on keeping their clients' attention riveted to the past—or, to a lesser degree, on the future. Doing so goes against common sense and against a key secret of happiness—*remain as much as possible in the present moment.* As Thoreau said, "Above all, we can not afford to not live in the present. He is blessed over all mortals who loses no moment of passing life in remembering the past."

It's my premise that therapy itself, or the goals of therapy, can be useful, if administered efficiently. This means treating a client within a reasonable period. Therapists need to teach useful skills to make people stronger, wiser, more able to experience the beauty in life—and less dependent on external sources such as therapists. A client should go into therapy, stress management, or any other personal growth-oriented process with clear objectives in mind. If you're a client or potential client, ask yourself these questions: "What is it I really want to get out of the process? What are my major goals? Do I want to be less confused or stressed? Do I want to be a better problem solver? Do I want better relationships? Do I want to be happier? Do I want to break a destructive habit? Do I want to learn better communication skills? What, exactly, do I want?" Once you know what you want, getting it will be easier.

The therapist, too, must have clear objectives. He or she must ask questions: "What do I want to teach this client? What is the best way to go about this goal?" A good therapist will be asking these questions frequently, likely before each meeting with the client. Why? Because the job of a therapist is to assist a client in achieving his or her stated objectives.

In my view, a major goal of any type of self-improvement therapy or process should be to learn to live, as much as possible, in the present moment. After all, the present is where life is actually lived. The past is over—even if the past you're concerned with is yesterday, or an hour ago. Likewise, the future is yet to be, whether you're concerned about next year or next week. Every personal goal you have can be enhanced by learning to live in the present. If you want to be happier, living in the present will help. If you want to solve problems more efficiently, living in the present will help. If you want to move on after experiencing grief, living in the present will help. If you want to have better personal relationships, living in the present will help. These and all other goals are enhanced by your ability to remain in the present moment. When your attention is right here, in the present, you're less distracted, more attentive, more focused, and more content.

Consider one of the major reasons you can read this book, or any book, and get something out of it. Isn't it in large part because you can keep your attention on what you're reading? How could you ever complete a book if you weren't able to maintain your concentration? Isn't it true that whenever you're responsive to the needs of others—whether an infant, a customer, or a friend in need—you're living in the present? Isn't it true that whenever you're effective at achieving any thing—reading a book, painting a picture, planting a garden—you're fully engaged in what you're doing, concentrating on the here and now? Happiness, relaxation, satisfaction, effectiveness, and compassion—in fact, all positive aspects of life—are found in the present moment. Thus, an obvious and important key to better living is to learn the art of living in the present.

People often feel stressed rather than more peaceful after extended periods of therapy because therapists' techniques and approaches take people *away* from the present moment, where inner peace is always found. Whenever your mind drifts away from the present by following trains of thought, you'll begin to lose your sense of contentment. Inner peace is a natural state of mind, but it can be found only in the absence of negative thinking. Whenever you're encouraged to think about something that bothers you, your sense of well-being will disappear.

How to Live in the Present Moment

Before I discuss how to live in the present, let me review what it *doesn't* involve. Living in the moment doesn't mean you're in denial about your past or present life. It doesn't mean you're apathetic about important issues, nor does it mean you aren't attentive to the problems in your life or compassionate about the needs of others. To the contrary; individuals who master the art of living in the present moment learn what it means to be levelheaded. They are sensitive to their own problems and the problems of others without becoming immobilized by them. They care about issues but realize that staying upset does nothing to improve a situation. They are passionate about certain topics but maintain just enough distance to keep a sense of perspective. And, as important, they don't lose sight of their major goal—to be content.

People who live in the present know that a contented state of mind not only feels better than any other state, but also that a levelheaded, contented mind is more effective and honest than a disturbed, frantic one. When you aren't distracted with thoughts about the past or future you are better able to make decisions. People who learn to live in the present moment end up being the kindest and most considerate people.

Why? Because when a person already has the satisfaction he or she wants out of life, there's something left over for other people. When you aren't always struggling to find meaning or happiness, it's easy to relate to others in a loving, giving way. A happy person is compassionate toward others because he knows what it's like to feel contentment and joy and can pass his loving feeling on to others. The person who is constantly feeling dissatisfied, distressed, struggling with his past and worrying about his future is usually unable to be kind and compassionate toward others. He is too consumed with his own wants and needs.

> *People who learn to live in the present moment get a great deal of what they want most out of life—satisfaction.*

Shirley's Story—She Feared the Future

Shirley has a nine-year-old daughter, named Candice, who has a slight mental handicap. Understandably, Shirley is concerned for her daughter's well-being. She went to therapy to gain support and to have someone to talk to about her feelings. A year later, she called my stress management center, claiming she felt far more stressed than she had before entering therapy. What happened?

Like many people in therapy, Shirley had been instructed to get in touch with her negative feelings, which she did. She was also convinced, at least initially, that it was in her best interest to continue to discuss "the issue" each week during her session. She did this too. Faithfully, each week, Shirley would talk about Candice, as well as her own fears, concerns, and worries. She would discuss the specific nature of Candice's problem, the details of what might go wrong in the future, and so on. A year later, she was a frantic and worried mother.

The "problem" had become paramount in her mind; she could think of little else. Her focus was now rarely on the present, but instead on her fearful thoughts of what might be later on. Her therapist insisted that she was being honest with her feelings and that this was a good thing.

It was important for Shirley to have someone to talk to. It may also have been important for her to be honest about her fears and concerns. But why did this process have to last a whole year? And, even more important, why didn't the process result in Shirley's becoming a more peaceful person?

I can't speak for everyone who has been through a similar process, and there may indeed be people who benefit from this kind of therapy, but in my opinion what Shirley needed most was to learn to live more of her life in the present moment. When Shirley was with Candice, all was well. Shirley wouldn't have changed anything about her daughter—her love for her was unconditional.

Shirley's distress came about when she allowed her mind to drift away from the present moment to her thoughts of fear about the future: "What if she never has a normal life? What's her life going to be like as an adult?" As her mind drifted from the present, and as she paid attention to her fearful thoughts, she felt the negative effect of those thoughts—the feeling of fear. As she learned to bring her attention back to the *now*, however, she quickly regained her perspective and her feeling of love for her daughter.

Consider this: When Shirley was with Candice, she felt a great deal of gratitude for having such a special child. The love she felt for her daughter was as strong as the love any parent has for a child. As long as her attention was directed to where she was or what she was doing, she was fine. In fact, she was better than fine, she was great.

Shirley learned to catch herself when her mind drifted too far from the present. She learned to detect non-present-moment-oriented thinking by the way she was feeling. Whenever she began to feel insecure or worried, it was a signal that she was once again allowing her mind to drift away from where she was.

You might be thinking, "Okay, this sounds fine, but doesn't Shirley need to attend to her daughter's needs? And, equally important, aren't her concerns valid?" The answer to both these questions is yes. The good news is, when your attention stays on what you're doing, and isn't distracted by thoughts of the past or the future, you are, very simply, at your personal best. Shirley's parenting skills flourished as her attention remained in the present. She was always able to respond in the most appropriate and loving manner.

Were Shirley's concerns valid? Of course they were. But there are two issues here. First is the legitimacy of her concerns. Shirley's prior therapist certainly helped her to realize that her concerns were valid. But the second issue, the one that is so often overlooked in therapy, is that of how Shirley related to what happened in her life.

This, in my opinion, is where Shirley's therapist failed her. Concern is warranted when you're faced with adversity, but what turns concern into something that immobilizes you is your willingness to drift away from the present moment— toward your thoughts of concern. Shirley's therapist helped her to acknowledge her pain and concern, but he didn't teach Shirley to free herself from being immobilized by it. He didn't teach her that her concern, legitimate as it was, was only present when her mind was focused on it. *At all other times,* she was free of the concern and its effects on her. By focusing on the present, Shirley learned that it's possible to maintain concern and commitment to difficulties without giving up happiness and contentment.

Many people are confused on this point. They believe that if you aren't visibly immobilized by the adversity you face, you're in denial about your problems or apathetic about life. This isn't so.

It's possible to maintain concern and commitment to difficulties without giving up happiness and contentment.

You can see that the details of Shirley's case are analogous to virtually all stressful situations. We all experience stress. Some people experience exceptionally stressful circumstances. But the dynamic that actually creates the stress you *feel* is something you have a great deal of control over. If you master the art of living in the present moment, you'll be able to handle far more stress than someone who allows his or her mind to drift to his or her concerns regularly.

Suppose you're confronted with the unfortunate experience of losing your job. At the same time, your best friend is confronted with the unfortunate experience of having her dinner guests stand her up. On the surface, it looks as though your situation is far more serious than your friend's. However, suppose your friend can't stop thinking about it. Each time a thought drifts into her consciousness about her rude guests, she unknowingly focuses her attention on her thoughts, creates more of them, and becomes discontented. You can see that it's probably only a matter of time before your friend drives herself crazy with this type of past-oriented thinking. Rather than redirecting her attention back to the present moment and recognizing that her unfortunate event is over and is now only a thought in her mind, she is trapped, as so many are, by her habit of following her negative trains of thought.

You, on the other hand, may have learned the art of present-moment living. You have learned the connection between your thinking and the way you feel. You know that whenever you follow a train of thought, especially when it's negative, you're likely to feel the effects of your thinking. You know that the loss of your job is a serious matter that must be dealt with, but you also know that to keep your perspective is critical, especially in this difficult time. By keeping your attention in the present moment, you'll allow your greatest wisdom to surface. As thoughts of "what now?" enter your mind, you dismiss them, not in denial, but in a conscious choice to remain calm. Dismissing your thoughts of negativity allows inspirational thoughts of wisdom to enter your mind, allowing you to take needed action.

Who is better off, you or your friend? I'd sure rather be in your shoes than those of your friend. Why? Because you have learned the art of happy living, even in the most difficult of times. If you can learn to keep your bearings in trying times, imagine how wonderful your life will be when times aren't so tough.

If you don't learn the art of present-moment living, your life won't go very smoothly, even when, on the surface, everything seems to be all right. Individuals who allow their minds to drift away from the present will find life difficult—regardless of their circumstances—because they will be in the habit of following, or focusing on, trains of thought, thus preventing wisdom from surfacing.

Begin to Live More of Your Life Now

The best way to begin living more of your life in the present moment is first to believe that it's a good idea. There is no specific technique to master and no fancy psychological theory to memorize. All that's needed is the knowledge that living in the moment is in your best interest and the desire to do so.

> *Living in the present isn't difficult or complicated, but it does take practice.*

If you're in the habit of allowing your mind to wander away from the moment, it will take some time to catch yourself doing so consistently. But persistence will pay off in the end.

Bob had what most people would consider a wonderful life. He is financially secure, healthy, physically fit, and engaged to be married. It's a habit of his, however, to follow negative trains of thought as they enter his mind. After realizing that he has been fortunate in life, for example, he might have a thought like "What if I lose my job?" Rather than recognizing that he has allowed his mind to slip out of the present, he focuses on his thought to the point of upsetting himself. If he does this often enough, his life, wonderful on the outside, will start to seem disappointing despite how fortunate he has been.

If Bob knows about the benefits of living in the present, he'll recognize that his mind has slipped away from the present moment toward an imagined future—and in this imagined future, he has innocently filled it with fear. His recognition of this gives him the choice to bring his attention back to the present, where his life is quite nice.

Some therapists would recommend that Bob get in touch with his fear of losing his job as well as his other self-doubting and pessimistic thoughts. Some therapists would encourage him to "feel his fear" and then think about the issue over and over again, encouraging more and similar thoughts. It's assumed that if a thought is present in the mind, it must be there for some hidden or important reason, and because of this, it must be addressed.

To this I say, nonsense! If you want to be a happier person, and if you want to move through therapy quickly, what you need to do is to get in touch with your positive feelings, not your most negative ones. Think about it. If you're unhappy, you're certainly already in touch with your negative feelings and out of touch with those that are positive. Remember, all unhappiness stems from the negative thoughts you have about your life, not from life itself. Once you're committed to this idea, many new options develop. As negative thoughts enter your mind you can dismiss them and think more positively.

If your thoughts are making you unhappy, they're not worth your attention.

As simple as living in the present may seem, it isn't always easy. And what's more, if you fail to learn the art of living in the present, you can turn even beautiful everyday experiences into negative situations. Let me give you two personal examples.

Recently I was driving to meet my mother (a former masters' marathon champion) for a date to go running. When I was about five minutes from our meeting place I began an internal dialogue with myself that went something like this: "It's been way too long since I met Mom for a run. I can't believe how quickly time flies. Here I am only a half-hour drive from her and I ask her to meet me for a run only a couple of times a year. What's wrong with me? Who knows how many more years this will even be an option? I should do this more often." On and on I went.

Rather than being grateful for the fact that the two of us were making time to exercise together, and rather than trying to enjoy the experience for what it was, I tortured myself with thoughts of regret without the slightest awareness of what I was doing.

Luckily I managed to catch myself about a minute before I got to my mom's, and the two of us had a good laugh about it. We then went out for a seven-mile run—and I was more tired than she was when we finished!

Another example is about a friend of mine who telephoned her mother, who lives in a different state. This friend has two small children and a great deal of responsibility, but she loves to keep in touch with her parents. She dialed the phone and here is what she heard: "Why haven't you called? I thought you crossed me off your list."

While this may sound amusing, it's quite a common experience. Rather than feeling joy at a phone call from her daughter, the mother felt angry and betrayed. Why does this happen? Does the mother in this example want to feel angry? Of course not. Her feelings are quite merely habitual. They stem from a simple case of misguided thinking. Rather than remaining in the present, where she was delighted to hear from her daughter, she let her thoughts (as I had done in the earlier example) drift backward from the moment, to the past few weeks when she hadn't received a call.

Your Everyday Life Is Special

When you live in the present moment, one of the nice things that happens to you is that ordinary, everyday life takes on a new significance. Taking walks, watching a sunset, gardening, reading a book, all begin to feel special. Life is right now, right here. When your attention is brought back to the here and now, you *engage* in life rather than think about life. Ordinary life becomes extraordinary life.

Let me share a funny story that demonstrates being touched by ordinary life. A friend and his wife were in Hawaii, standing on a beach, watching a beautiful sunset—hardly able to believe how magnificent the sight was. A woman approached them and overhead my friend's wife say, "I can't believe how beautiful this is." While walking away from the spectacular display, the woman replied, "You should have seen it in Tahiti."

When your attention isn't on the present moment but on something else, you'll tend to compare even good experiences with others, as the Tahiti traveler did, or you'll wonder about future experiences instead of enjoying the present one, and regret past experiences because they're already over. But as you learn to bring your attention back to the here and now, life will come alive again, providing the enjoyment and satisfaction it was meant to.

If each moment is lived to its fullest, your future will be well cared for when it eventually does arrive.

I have been criticized at times for being too simplistic in my approach to happier living. People find it difficult to believe that simple solutions can be so effective. I remain steadfast, however, in my belief that solutions such as learning to live in the present not only can be helpful but also represent most of what you need to know to live a happy, productive life. The previous two simple examples demonstrate the beauty and wisdom of living in the present moment. It's simple, but it works! If your mind can sabotage even beautiful experiences, such as spending time with or receiving a phone call from someone you love, you can imagine how easy it can be to ruin your life over events and circumstances that are, in fact, difficult. It's critical to learn to live in the present.

You need not worry that you'll lose any effectiveness in making plans for the future if you aren't focused on it. Life is a series of present moments, one right after another. Living them to the full prepares the future. What's more, when the future does arrive, you will have learned and practiced how to live in the present moment and you'll be able to enjoy your future as much as you can enjoy today.

PRINCIPLE SEVEN:
Dig Deep for Your Wisdom

There is no happiness where there is no wisdom.

—SOPHOCLES

Throughout this book I have discussed the importance of learning to distrust your thinking when it gets in your own way, when it immobilizes you. We have looked at the nature of thought: what it is, how it affects us, how it can become an obstacle, even ruin our lives. Like many people learning these principles for the first time, you may wonder how to tell which of your thoughts you should pay attention to and which ones to dismiss.

We're fortunate to have within ourselves an inner intelligence that is deeper and more profound than any test could ever measure—wisdom. Although we have experienced our own wisdom on many occasions, we often fail to recognize its existence in our lives, and most of us never really learn to gain access to our wisdom at will.

> **Wisdom exists outside the confines of our ordinary frame of reference.**

When we tap into our wisdom we aren't thinking in the usual sense, but perceiving things from an entirely different standpoint. Our experience of our individual circumstances varies tremendously—depending on whether we're seeing life from a state of wisdom or from an ordinary, business-as-usual model.

Perhaps wisdom seems difficult to tap into regularly because it's an invisible force within. Unlike ordinary intellectual thinking, which can be quantified, pointed to, and discussed, wisdom is a silent voice that exists only when thinking is turned off. It's much easier to discuss what's on your mind than what's in your heart. However, it's quite possible to access your wisdom. And when you learn to do so, your life will begin to run more smoothly, answers to questions will begin to surface, and life will take on new significance.

If you want to move through therapy quickly, or if you want to get out of therapy altogether, you must learn to find and trust your own inner wisdom. For that matter, if you want to live a joyful, contented life, learning to trust your wisdom is not only a shortcut but a prerequisite. The reason: Wisdom is the guiding force in your life, the tool that helps you navigate in the most appropriate direction. It teaches you what to focus on and contemplate, what actions to take, and what to ignore.

How Does Your Wisdom Work?

Let's look at a simple, common example of how wisdom might work in your life. Suppose you're at a close friend's house attending a dinner party in your honor. Your friend is serving magnificent food and has made elaborate preparations. Furthermore, let's suppose you weren't feeling very well when you arrived, and as delicious as the food is, each bite increases the queasy feeling in your stomach.

Clearly you have to make a decision. You're having a wonderful time. Your friend has prepared a wonderful meal just for you. The food is beautifully displayed and looks to have been quite expensive, probably more than your thoughtful host can realistically afford. To compound matters, you've always believed that to waste food is a crime. It's important to eat everything on your plate.

A voice within tells you to stop eating. You sense that you should listen to this voice, but you hesitate. Why? Because, on the surface, it looks as though it might be more trouble than it's worth to listen. After all, you're not certain you'll get sick if you continue eating—there's no guarantee. Further, what about your friend's feelings? Wouldn't she be crushed if you didn't eat everything? What about all the trouble she went through just for you? Wouldn't it be insensitive to stop eating—however good the reason might be? But that inner voice keeps reminding you to stop, telling you that if you continue you'll pay a high price.

What do you do? Do you take a chance? Do you risk hurting your friend's feelings? What you do is listen to your wisdom and find a way to take care of yourself, while at the same time acting sensitively to your friend's feelings.

It's not always easy to follow the guidance of your wisdom. Sometimes your wisdom gives you difficult advice—on changing careers or partners, disciplining your children, altering your diet, quitting a bad habit. But the guidance is always there. There's always a part of you—if you listen—that knows exactly what you need to do.

> **Wisdom is a simple, quiet sense of knowing what is right for you.**

A client recently told me a story about how his wisdom may have saved his life, or at least kept him out of jail. He was drinking champagne at a party—too much champagne—when the group decided to move to a new location. As much fun as he was having with his friends, something inside him reminded him that he had already had too much to drink and shouldn't drive. Though he needed his car the next day and couldn't easily afford a taxi, he listened to his wisdom—even through the obvious effects of too much alcohol—and called a cab. Fifteen minutes into the cab ride, he passed out. If he had been driving, who knows what might have happened?

Listening to your wisdom instead of your thoughts can produce dramatic effects. At other times, the effects are far more subtle. Sometimes, you'll never know what might have happened if you hadn't listened to and responded with wisdom. In the two examples above this was clearly the case.

But that's the nature of wisdom—it's mysterious. Often the voice of wisdom is subtle, quiet, even inexplicable. While you can't always put your finger on exactly what it is, it's still there—guiding you—if you learn to trust it.

When you think of the word *wisdom,* it can, at times, conjure up images of "new age thinking," and sound like something credible people don't rely on. We've come to revere the use of the intellect; the smarter a person seems to be, the more he or she is respected. In reality, this view of wisdom is false and misguided. Wisdom is a calm yet confident feeling of knowing what to do and how to do it. It is the source of your intuition and creativity and what allows one to attain happiness.

Some of the more difficult clients I've worked with have been the most intelligent, in the narrow sense of the word. This is often true not because there's anything inherently wrong with intelligence, but because many people rely on and trust their intelligence only to guide them in all matters. Because they rely on intelligence and logic, they attempt to "figure out" their life. In so doing, however, they get caught up in their own thinking about issues rather than trying to find solutions.

Analysis Paralysis

Regardless of your individual IQ, if you have been in longterm therapy you have undoubtedly fallen into the trap of using your own intelligence against yourself. I call this tendency analysis paralysis. Simply put, this is the result of getting caught up in your own mind and then trying to think your way out of your self-created trap.

> **It's possible to be a very intelligent person, yet have very little wisdom.**

Here's an example of analysis paralysis that comes from a superintelligent, successful client of mine, a businesswoman named Kim. Kim is a major decision maker for her company. She must continually review options and recommend action for her employer.

Kim was in the habit of mentally reviewing her choices over and over again. She would peruse the same set of facts hundreds of times. She would analyze the data, go over the options with a fine-toothed comb, and then review her assessment once again. She couldn't sleep because she couldn't stop thinking about her choices. Kim would make her ultimate decision moments before her deadline—because she would simply run out of time.

When I asked Kim about her track record regarding the results of her decisions, she claimed it was terrific. In other words, despite almost killing herself with her own thinking, the end result was positive. Like other extremely intelligent clients I have worked with, Kim used her excellent results to justify her decision-making process. Because she was so result-oriented, she never questioned her method.

Kim's problem wasn't her ability to make good decisions, but rather her tendency to get caught up in her mind and feel stressed out. She needed to try a different method. I asked her to consider how much good she was going to do her company if she expired from stress. "Being dead is bad for business," I told her. Although she laughed, she became interested in what I had to say.

I taught Kim to have this goal: to focus on the part of

her that wasn't thinking—that is, the "space" between her thoughts, the quiet part of her mind, her wisdom. Of course, this was a very abstract concept to her, but she gave it a try. She learned that she could have a series of thoughts—even brilliant ones—yet create some distance from those thoughts to give her wisdom some room to surface. She learned that doing so wouldn't jeopardize her brilliance; in fact, it would increase it.

Kim discovered that being caught up in her thinking wasn't to her ultimate advantage. She later came to the conclusion that she made good business decisions not because of her tendency to overevaluate her options but *despite* this tendency. She learned to detect when she was caught up by stressful feelings. Instead of diving in and thinking even more when she was feeling stressed, as she was accustomed to doing, she learned to back off from her thinking instead.

As is often the case, it turned out that Kim usually knew which decision to make about a minute after reviewing her options. Her initial "hunch," almost without exception, turned out to be the decision she made—sometimes a week later. The quality of her decisions didn't change after she learned to trust her wisdom. What changed was the amount and type of mental activity required and the amount of stress she felt.

Keep Your Thinking Machine Well Oiled

Once in a while, someone I work with asks me if I advocate not thinking. I do not! It's important to realize that backing off from your thinking doesn't mean you stop thinking. It simply means slowing down, pacing yourself, and taking a break. An analogy that works for me is to think of a rock or gravel funnel that is sifting and separating different types of rocks. The funnel can allow only a certain amount of material to travel through it at any moment. If the opening of the funnel gets clogged, the machine breaks down and stops working. If you respond to the clogging by trying to stuff even more material into the opening, you compound the problem instead of solving it. The solution is to remove some of the material that is trying to get through the opening. Once you do, everything starts working again.

There is a limited amount of thought that can exist in your mind at any moment. Just as with the sifting machine, too much material (too many thoughts) clogs the mechanism and interferes with its operation. Once your mind is on overload, adding more thoughts increases the stress and makes matters worse. The solution is to back off for a minute, take a break, regain your perspective, and allow your "thought machine" to kick back into gear on its own.

A rock-sifting machine has a mechanism that keeps it from getting clogged. When the machine's opening becomes filled up, a signal alerts the operator of the machine to slow down the pace. If the operator of the machine listens and responds appropriately to the warning signal, the machine continues to perform at its best.

Human beings have an equally effective mechanism to alert us when our thinking is getting clogged, when our mind isn't working as well as it could—stress. As with the sifting machine, when we're functioning optimally, the warning signal is silent. This means that no adjustments need to be made; everything is operating as it should. When the alarm goes off, it means there is a problem—but also a solution.

The human warning signal is loud and clear and it works perfectly every time. There are, however, many times in life when the human thinking machine fails to listen or respond to the warning signal. When you do this, your thinking gets more and more clogged, and as you attempt to think your way out, you only add to the problem. There is simply too much mental activity.

The best response to your warning signal is to recognize that there is too much mental activity; you're caught up in your own thinking. This recognition alone allows you to take a step back—almost like taking your foot off a gas pedal. Very little effort is involved. Just a gentle backing off, a clearing of the mind, allows your thinking to regain its best pace. Wisdom then can present itself.

When you pay attention to this warning signal (the stressed-out way you're feeling), you decrease the stress in your life and facilitate your ability to get at your wisdom. You already have the wisdom you need inside you. To bring it forth, you simply need to get out of your own way.

Matters of the Heart Need Your Wisdom

At times, your intellect can actually get in the way of making simple choices in your life, or solving certain types of problems, particularly in matters of the heart.

These are characterized by their personal nature; they are problems or decisions that require intuition and wisdom. You may need to reach a decision about marriage or career, or about discussing sex or drugs with your teenager. Unless you understand and value your wisdom, you have no alternative but to call on your intellect to deal with your personal issues.

I love this simple story, because it illustrates this point so well. In New York City the driver of a big delivery truck tried to drive under an overpass despite posted warnings that his truck was too tall. The signs were right; the top of the truck smashed into the overpass, and the truck got stuck. There was panic, and the city officials called in highly paid experts in architecture and engineering. They studied the situation for the better part of a day, trying to determine the best course of action, the best angles to try to pry the truck free without damaging the overpass.

Although the area was sealed off, a six-year-old boy walked up to the scene and tugged on a police officer's pants, trying to get his attention. "Leave me alone, kid, can't you see we've got important work to do here?" "But mister," the little boy insisted, "why don't you let the air out of the tires?"

Sometimes the answers we're looking for are obvious—if we could somehow get out of our own way and listen to what they are, turn off the thinking mind, and know that an appropriate answer is within reach. When you understand that your wisdom always can and will provide you with appropriate and valuable answers, you feel an enormous sense of relief.

Many times each day, I sit back and wait for an answer, even when I'm under some sort of deadline. My wisdom will act more quickly and less stressfully than my brain will. Whether I'm coming up with a title for a book or an article, trying to remember someone's name or phone number, considering a plan of action for one of my children, or trying to decide on a new place for a family vacation, I attempt to rely on my wisdom to be my guiding force. When I do, I'm always satisfied with the results.

If you ask (as I have) a hundred people the question "What is more important—what you know, or how you feel?" almost all will respond, "How I feel is more important." But as universally true as this seems to be, virtually all the emphasis in what we're taught is on the cognitive, the "what you know" aspect of life. It's not that this aspect isn't critical—it is. But learning to deal with matters of the heart in appropriate and effective ways is usually left out of the picture—even though they're the most important aspect of life to most of us. No doubt, if we learned to use our wisdom a little more often and our thinking minds a little less often, we would have far fewer social problems—families would be stronger, marriages would be more loving, drugs and alcohol would be less tempting, and kindness would be more common.

Once you know that your wisdom lies within you, all that's required to gain access to it is your intention to do so and your willingness to quiet down your thinking mind.

> *If you think of your wisdom as another type of intelligence, you can learn to call on it more regularly.*

Traditional Therapy Needs More Wisdom

One problem I see in so-called traditional therapy is that therapists more often than not use only the intellect to solve problems or to work through issues. In other words, therapists often encourage us to solve problems by the same process that created them.

Einstein once said, "We will never solve the problems of the world at the same level of understanding that created them." I believe he meant that to change, we must view things in an entirely different light—we must rise above our problems and see them freshly. We must look at life through the eyes of our wisdom instead of relying on our business-as-usual way of looking at life.

To make positive changes in your life, to achieve greater contentment, or to solve a specific problem, you must have a change of heart—you must see the situation in a new light, see the facts in a different way. For a troubled marriage to get better, for example, the couple involved must rise above, step outside their existing frame of reference, in which they view each other in a negative light, and learn to see other, more positive dimensions of each other and of the relationship. William James, the father of American psychology once said, "Wisdom is nothing more than seeing things in a nonhabitual way." It's the ability to step back from your usual way of seeing life and of doing things. This becomes easier as your mind quiets down.

Try to remember a time when you made a decision that felt right even though it might have seemed wrong to other people. The decision may or may not have made sense from an intellectual standpoint, but you knew what was right for you. You changed careers even though you seemed to be on track, you had a baby even though everyone thought you were too young (or too old), or you took up a new hobby or challenge no one else thought you should try.

Of course, it's not necessarily the case that you're using your wisdom simply because you're making what looks to be a silly decision. It may be that you're simply trying to rationalize a rebellious act in the name of wisdom. In the examples above, a person might *not* be using his or her wisdom at all but instead be demonstrating dysfunctional thinking that could lead to hardship and emotional pain.

To determine whether you are using wisdom, you must make an honest assessment of how you feel when you make the decision. Are you hesitant? Do you feel awkward? Or do you just *know* inside that the decision is the right one? If so, it's your wisdom speaking, that feeling that "this is right."

Your Inner Wisdom Is an Important Shortcut

You may be pleasantly surprised at how quickly you can learn to use and trust your own wisdom—precisely why I have included it as a shortcut through therapy. When you learn to rely on your wisdom, it makes anything you would go into therapy for much easier to deal with and far less complicated: Most problems can be solved more effectively and with less stress, sound decisions can be made, and most destructive patterns or tendencies you may have can be detected and changed.

Your wisdom is an important key to living a life you can be proud of—and grateful for. Learning to trust your wisdom is a statement to yourself that ultimately only you can decide what's best for you. Your wisdom is like a navigational instrument that can guide you through life. When you discover and listen to your wisdom, many of the answers to the issues and concerns you went into therapy for will become apparent. You'll see that life isn't always as complicated as your therapist believes it has to be.

PRINCIPLE EIGHT:
Count Your Blessings

Learn appreciation. You won't be happy with more until you are happy with what you've got.

—VIKI KING

Regardless of how much time you spent in therapy, you would never *feel* the value of therapy, would never reap the fruits of your labor, unless you were able to cultivate a sense of gratitude in your life. Why? Because the feeling of gratitude is a foundation of personal contentment, satisfaction, and the ability to enjoy life. Gratitude is a powerful antidote to virtually all stress, unhappiness, and frustration.

Learning to feel grateful is a shortcut through therapy. Often, the focus in therapy is on how you can change your life in order to feel gratitude. In this chapter we'll reverse this process. I'll show you how to feel gratitude now, without changing anything in your life. You'll feel grateful for the way your life is right now. This gratitude, in turn, will aid you in making any changes that would improve your life. In short, it's a lot quicker and more efficient to learn the art of gratitude than to attempt to rearrange your life in a particular way *so that* you can feel gratitude.

Throughout history, wise men and woman have urged us to feel grateful for what we have. Why? Very simply because gratitude makes us feel good. When you're feeling grateful, your mind is clear, and therefore you have access to your greatest wisdom and common sense. You see the big picture. You make wise decisions. You look back on painful events with greater perspective and you look forward to likely events with less fear. If you were able to feel gratitude instead of the desire for things to be other than they are, as most of us do, your life would not only feel good, but it would run very smoothly as well.

People are most fulfilled when they rejoice in what they have. Those who live the least fulfilling lives are constantly complaining about what's wrong with their lives or what's missing—regardless of how good their lives may appear. How can we explain the fact that many people with apparently difficult lives feel a tremendous gratitude, and consequently enjoy their lives, while many others with apparently fortunate lives feel no gratitude whatsoever—and therefore fail to enjoy theirs? The answer to this question is that gratitude is an attitude. It has nothing whatsoever to do with what we have or don't have, and everything to do with the attitude we take toward life.

It's only a habit, a way of thinking about life, that prevents you from feeling gratitude. How often have you fallen into the trap of focusing your attention on the one or two areas of your life that aren't yet perfect? How often do you think to yourself, "My life would be better if only . . . ," instead of marveling at how wonderful so much of your life already is? If you can learn to shift your attention away from what would make your existing life better and focus instead on the beauty of life as it is, you will have learned a key component of happy, productive living.

Appreciate the Power of Your Thinking

As with other shortcuts through therapy, this one depends on your understanding of the central role of thought in your life. Recall the chain of events that occurs when you have a thought:

(1) You think. (2) You feel the effects of that thought. For example, if you have the thought "My life isn't all that great. It would be better if . . . ," you will instantly begin to feel a little defeated or pessimistic. This chain reaction *always* happens, which as I said before tells you that it's not really your life that's not all that great, but the fact that you're having negative thoughts *about* your life, focusing on them, believing them to be true. This chain of events occurs so quickly that it can make you believe that your life isn't very good. If you have these types of thoughts and believed them to be true, you would feel bad about your life irrespective of what your life looked like on the outside. You could be a millionaire, live a comfortable life with your ideal mate, and have all your dreams come true. But if you combined this dream life with unchecked negativity, all your gratitude would quickly disappear, and along with it all your happiness. Your unhappiness would remain until you learned to dismiss these types of thoughts from your mind—as simply thoughts.

> *People who live the most fulfilling lives are the ones who are always rejoicing at what they have.*

To regain or achieve a sense of gratitude in your life, you *must* begin to appreciate the power your own thinking has over the way you feel. If you harbor negative thoughts, for whatever reason, *you* are going to be the person who feels that negativity, the opposite of gratitude. If you're angry at someone, you feel the anger. If you're jealous, you feel the jealous feelings. If you're suspicious, you are the owner of that feeling as well. And when these feelings are present, the feeling of gratitude disappears.

As I've said, many people believe erroneously that it's somehow important to think about the negative aspects of your life. The rationale for this belief is that by doing so you will acknowledge and sort out your most honest and legitimate feelings, the assumption being that your negative feelings are the ones that matter.

The problem with this belief is that feelings don't exist on their own. They are created from moment to moment by the way you think about life and by how much you believe in your thoughts. There are no negative feelings stored up inside your body or mind. Negativity isn't hiding in your genes waiting for its chance to jump out and ruin your life, nor is pessimism an inherited trait. Instead, you create negativity, or squelch your sense of gratitude, when you think about something in your life in a negative way and believe your thoughts to be true. It's *the act of thinking* combined with your belief in your thoughts that takes away your sense of gratitude.

Joan's and Ann's Stories

Joan has a single negative thought that she believes to be true: "Life is really hard." She focuses on this thought most of the time when it is present in her mind. She believes that because her life is hard, it's inappropriate and unrealistic to feel grateful. She decides she'll feel grateful only if and when her life, on an external level, has fewer difficulties. Joan feels quite unhappy—despite being talented, employed, beautiful, young, and newly married to a man who loves and respects her.

Ann, on the other hand, has learned to dismiss or ignore her negative thoughts even though her negativity seems more justified. Ann's husband of many years has recently left her. She has three children to care for, and few marketable job skills. She also struggles with a slight physical handicap. Here is a small sample of her frequent negative thoughts before working with me: "I hate Dave (her ex-husband); I'll never get out of this one; I hate my life; I'm too old for this." In short, she had been seeing herself as a victim.

Despite outward appearances of a difficult and challenging life and the total acknowledgment of her negative thoughts (she isn't trying to fool herself or anyone else), Ann has now broken her habit of focusing on the troublesome aspects of her life. She told me she realized that any attention given to her negativity resulted in an instant loss of any gratitude she had felt for her life, her children, or her future.

The comparison of these two woman shows that the content of our thinking is secondary. It simply represents the details of what we happen to be thinking about. The important issue is how much emphasis we put on these thoughts. In other words, do we focus on them and believe in them simply because they have come to mind—and because we're in the habit of doing so? Or can we see our thoughts of negativity distracting us from our feelings of gratitude?

Despite an outwardly ideal life, Joan has put a great deal of emphasis on her single thought, "Life is hard," thus feeling the effects of her negativity strongly. Ann, on the other hand, has learned to dismiss her negative thoughts, not out of conscious or unconscious denial, but simply because doing so brings gratitude back into her life quickly. Ann knows that when she feels gratitude for what she already has, it's much easier for her to make decisions from a place of wisdom— decisions that will ultimately improve her life, and the lives of her children, and make her even happier. Then she will have even more to be grateful for—along with being an excellent role model for her children.

Gratitude Through Traditional or Shortcut Therapy?

As was discussed in chapter 3, the emphasis in therapy usually goes to the specific details of the client's thoughts. In this example, had these two women been in traditional therapy, who would have been better suited? Joan, of course. Why? Because she had only one main negative thought. Ann, on the other hand, would have been in big trouble. She in all likelihood would have been encouraged to "work through" each negative thought individually by examining it and focusing on it. Instead of dismissing her thoughts, Ann would have been encouraged to entertain them and work through them.

When examining which therapy model makes more sense, go back to the central questions: "What am I looking for?" and "What do I want out of life?" Chances are you're looking for inner peace, contentment, happiness, and the ability to solve problems efficiently. If this is indeed the case, the next question to ask yourself is "How am I going to achieve these goals?" Will you achieve happiness by focusing on your pain? Will you feel gratitude by assuming that your most negative, low-mood thoughts are the ones to become aware of? Or does it make more sense to acknowledge that you're going to have plenty of negative thoughts to contend with, as well as plenty of low moods, and the key to happiness is to learn how to deal with them? If you can learn to set aside your negativity, banishing it from the forefront of your mind, you'll be able to call up a feeling of gratitude.

I have seen clients similar to Joan who, in my opinion, had nothing wrong with their lives other than a bad habit of focusing on their stray negative thoughts and taking them too seriously. Some of these clients had become convinced, with the help of their therapists, that they had a deep, serious problem that must be dealt with. Sometimes this led to several years of therapy—when all the client really wanted and needed was to feel more gratitude for his or her life. I have yet to see any of these clients emerge from this process feeling more gratitude or more satisfaction.

Obviously there are times when a client really does have a serious problem and professional help may be required. In no way am I suggesting that every issue in life can be dealt with by simply ignoring your thoughts on the subject so that you can regain your feeling of gratitude. What I am suggesting is that *you feel the way you do because of the thoughts you're thinking.* If you're feeling ungrateful, that means you're having negative thoughts that you're taking too seriously. This will be true even if you believe that the thoughts you're having are justified, which you undoubtedly will most of the time.

If someone you love is in an accident, you're probably going to feel grief and sadness. Even though you're certainly justified in feeling this way, it's still true that the attention you give to your thoughts about the incident determines the way you feel. It's also true that if you were able to shift your thinking away from sadness and focus instead on whatever thoughts of gratitude you have for your injured friend—if you could think, for example, of how lucky you are even to know your friend—you would begin to experience a change in your overall frame of mind—a change for the better, even within difficult circumstances.

Dinah's Story—The Price for Negative Thoughts Was Too High

Dinah was constantly dissatisfied with her life. She believed the only way to deal with it was to think about it and try to solve her problems. One dissatisfaction she expressed constantly concerned her career. Her strategy was to continue changing careers until she found the right one. When asked why she had yet to find a career she enjoyed, her response was "I haven't had enough opportunities yet." She had changed jobs at least once a year for almost ten years. Another dissatisfaction was her relationships with men. Although she claimed she wanted to settle down, she had had seven boyfriends in three years.

The great challenge for Dinah was to understand the idea that her dissatisfaction was something she created within her own mind. It resulted from paying attention to her negative thoughts to the point of removing her sense of gratitude. If not for thoughts like "I hate this job," the feeling of job dissatisfaction could not and would not exist. This doesn't mean it's never appropriate to change jobs or relationships; it most certainly is. What it means is that you shouldn't allow changing jobs to interfere with the quality of your life on the whole.

Consider the following chart, which aided Dinah considerably in regaining her gratitude for life:

THOUGHT→FEELING→BEHAVIOR

You have a thought. This thought leads to a feeling, which can then lead to various types of behavior. For example, Dinah had the thought "I couldn't possibly feel grateful. My job is boring."

Notice, however, that there is a space between thought and feeling, and another between feeling and behavior. The spaces represent where your potential wisdom lies. Or, if you're not careful, those spaces can just as easily be your source of potential insanity.

There is a moment after each thought, and between series of thoughts, in which you have the opportunity to respond or not respond to what has just occurred. Do you say to yourself or respond unconsciously by feeling this way: "Oh no, an important thought. I have to take it seriously. I must act now." Do you respond to each thought as if it were an emergency? Or do you simply acknowledge that you just had a thought about something and now have the choice to act on it, ignore it, dismiss it, or reconsider it later on?

The answers to these questions are important to your mental health and to your ability to cultivate gratitude in your life.

If you believe that the thoughts that form in your mind need to be examined and taken seriously, you should reconsider. If you can learn that thoughts don't need to be taken too seriously, and can be looked at with perspective, from a distance, you can regain control over your own life—and gratitude will quickly emerge. If you enter therapy with this deeper perspective, there will be an end in sight; you'll have discovered a shortcut.

Dinah was quick to learn that her thoughts were like a tape playing in her mind. They just keep coming and going. She learned that while she sometimes had little if any control over which thoughts entered her mind, she had enormous control over which thoughts she took seriously and which ones she ignored. She decided that the price for paying attention to her negative thoughts was, in her words, "far too high."

Focus on What You Already Have Instead of What You Want

Most of us spend a great deal of time and energy thinking about, focusing on, and wishing for what we want. We do this for one simple reason: We believe that if we get what we want, we'll feel satisfied and happy. But this really isn't so. Think back to all the times in your life when you did get what you wanted; if you're like most people, you still feel unsatisfied. You grew up, you received a diploma, you earned rewards, you received a promotion, you raised a family, you improved your physical fitness, you found your lost pet. The point is that hundreds, even thousands of times in your life, you have received exactly what you hoped for, yet the happiness you seek still eludes you. Why?

Happiness comes about as the result of lessening the gap between what you have and what you want. But you'll never get there if, each time you get what you want, you allow your attention to drift once again toward what would be even better. This drifting mind is the vehicle that takes you away from gratitude.

You can only feel happy if you shift your focus from what you think would give you happiness and pay attention to what you have. When you do, you'll get the great feeling you've been looking for. Despite how obvious this seems, most of us do just the opposite. Instead of learning to appreciate what we have, we continue believing that the next fulfilled desire or the next achievement will be different. The *next one* really will bring us joy!

*Ultimately, the only way to feel happy is to stop fo-
cusing your attention on what you think would make
you happy and be happy with what you have.*

If your mind is in the habit of focusing on what you want
instead of what you already have, you'll always feel dissatisfied
regardless of what you get. You could win ten million dollars
in the lottery and still feel dissatisfied or worried if your attention stayed on the taxes the government would be taking out
of your winnings. It's where you place your attention that
determines how you're going to feel—not what you end up ac-
quiring or achieving. Again, this doesn't mean it's inappropriate or unnecessary to strive toward goals, but it does suggest
that achieving them won't bring you happiness—unless you
learn to feel gratitude for what you already have.

Perhaps the most ironic part of this understanding is that
when you focus on what you have instead of what you want,
you end up getting more of what you want anyway. It work this
way: The gratitude that develops acts as positive energy, or
fuel, that leads toward your heart's desire. Optimism leads to
satisfaction, which encourages you to take action and look for
more positive aspects in your life. Negativity, or focusing your
energy on what's lacking in your life, only encourages you to
find more of the same. It's impossible to feel satisfied. What's
more, your negative attention will act as negative fuel, encouraging you to focus on mistakes and pitfalls, which means you'll
end up getting less of what you want. The best way to learn
the art of gratitude is to practice ignoring or dismissing the
thoughts you have that interfere with this feeling. Consider
the following example.

Steve's Story—He Learned to Work with Far Less Stress

Steve was a client who insisted he "couldn't afford to be grateful." He came to my stress management center because of job burnout. When I asked him what he meant by not being able to afford to be grateful, he said, "If I feel gratitude it means that I'm satisfied with where I already am—and I'm not. I want to excel and achieve in my life. It sounds to me like you're suggesting that I roll over and simply feel happy."

"Why do you want to achieve?" I asked.

"Because achieving makes me happy," he responded.

I continued by asking him, "But what if you could feel happy right now, *before* you achieved anything. Would that be okay?"

"Well, sure," he said, "but then I'd stop achieving."

Back in chapter 1, I discussed the notion of "as if" realities. Steve was living as if there were a connection between feeling satisfied and a lack of success. He believed that feeling gratitude was tantamount to a prescription for apathy, and that inner struggle was his path to success.

One key in working with Steve was for him to have the experience of what his own wisdom felt like. He practiced ignoring thoughts like these: "I'll be happy when . . . ," "Tomorrow life will be better," and "I can't afford to rest." He had been unfamiliar with what life felt like without these thoughts, and he was pleasantly surprised. In the absence of a head full of tiring, dictatorial thoughts, he learned to feel a sense of relaxation and ease, and he found that achieving this state of mind was far simpler than he could have imagined.

The process Steve went through consisted of two very simple steps. First, he needed to understand that gratitude is his most natural state. This means that in the absence of interference (negative thoughts), he would feel a pleasant sense of gratitude. To verify this for yourself, think of how you were as a child. Can you remember how excited you felt about simple little things? Just this morning, my five-year-old daughter spent over two hours planting apple seeds in the dirt. Her two-year-old sister was busy collecting rocks! Do you remember how easy it was to be touched by ordinary life? If not, make a point of spending some time around small kids—not to become childish, but to remember how it feels to be childlike. Steve learned that he, like everyone else, naturally felt grateful at one time in his life. He had simply learned to feel ungrateful.

The second step was for Steve to practice the art of dismissing the thoughts that interfered with his feelings of gratitude. At first, as is true with many clients, he felt he was dismissing most of the thoughts that entered his mind. "They're all negative," he insisted when he called me on the phone the evening after our first session together. "That's okay," I told him, "keep dismissing them. They'll start to go away." Steve did keep dismissing them. And within a few sometimes discouraging days, he had got into the habit of dismissing the negative thoughts that used to fill his head.

The first question I asked him during his next session was "What's it like now?" "It's really weird," he responded. "My mind seems rather empty, yet I'm a lot happier." "Well, have you turned into a beach bum yet?" I asked. After laughing out loud, Steve responded by admitting, "Hardly. In fact, I've gotten the same amount of work done, if not more. But the funny thing is I'm not tired after work like I used to be. I don't feel the same amount of stress."

One of the things that turned Steve around was to realize that it was in his own best interest to learn the art of gratitude. This was true not only so that he could be a happier person, but so that he could achieve his goals. Despite the common belief that we work better under stress, most of us actually work better when the pressure is off.

When Your Mind Is Clear, You Can See the Bigger Picture

When your mind isn't distracted by thoughts and you don't feel fearful, a greater amount of wisdom, common sense, and creative genius presents itself. This isn't to say deadlines or rewards can't be helpful in terms of motivation, but it does suggest that your end result will be more complete, less habitual, and more creative when your mind is free—when you're feeling contented and grateful.

> *Often we come to believe that we work better under stress only because we don't have a strong sense of what it's like not to feel stress.*

This was certainly the case with Steve. He insisted he could only work "under stress or duress," yet he learned that this simply wasn't true. He had to admit (and was delighted to do so) that he had no idea what it felt like to work free of this distraction. In fact, he shared with me some wisdom that I in turn, would like to share with you: "Believing that emotional stress is necessary for success is like believing that a sprained ankle is necessary for winning a foot race."

Robin's Story—Gratitude Healed Her

This applies to more serious cases too, as the following story demonstrates.

Robin was raped by a man she was out on a date with. It was the most horrifying, degrading experience of her life. She came to my office in tears, saying, "My life is ruined." She had experienced what many women fear most.

Anyone, regardless how bad circumstances might seem, can learn to feel grateful for her life once she sees how gratitude works for her. In other words, seeing the importance and relevance of gratitude is the first step in the development of gratitude, even through the most distressing times. In fact, gratitude is the factor that can best help you get through difficult times intact.

Robin's first hurdle was to overcome her insistence that she could never again feel gratitude in her life. She needed to see that gratitude could relieve her emotional pain as a therapeutic massage might relieve a backache. While you're having a massage, the pain diminishes, but often once it's over, the pain returns. Likewise, when your mind slips out of a state of gratitude and returns to a state of worry, concern, anger, or regret, the memory of your hurtful emotional experience begins to have a greater effect on you again.

Robin heard my initial pitch for the cultivation of gratitude with curiosity, along with understandable hesitation. She asked me, "Are you saying that if I were to feel gratitude instead of my existing feelings, my stress and negative feelings would go away?"

"Not really," I said, "only that it would be greatly reduced. I'm saying that, in time, you can learn to recharacterize your experience in a slightly different way—a way that includes gratitude for the fact that you weren't seriously physically hurt and that you're okay today. I'm also saying that I know you have it in you, *and* that you deserve to be happy. God knows you've already been through enough pain. You told me that your therapist said it was important for you to acknowledge your feelings and to stay out of denial about this. To a large degree, I agree with her. But remember, I'm not your therapist. You came to me because you were already in therapy and it didn't help you feel any better—you wanted a shortcut to feeling better.

"I'm here to teach you to empower yourself into feeling far less stress and far more happiness. You *can* do this if you understand the awesome nurturing power of gratitude. I guess the difference between the approach I intend to teach you and the approach your therapist was using is that my single goal is for you to learn to use your mind in a way that will give you your power back. Are you with me so far?"

"Yes," she said.

Like many clients, Robin was surprised that during our next several sessions together, we never once discussed the incident that prompted her to visit me in the first place. At one point, she asked me, "Do you realize that we haven't spoken of my rape at all?"

"Yes, of course. Do you mind?"

"No," she answered, "not at all. It just seems curious."

"Do you have any new ideas as to why we haven't been discussing your rape? Do you think I've been trying to keep you in denial?"

She laughed (she hadn't even smiled before) and said, "It's funny, I don't feel at all in denial, but I am beginning to feel a little better."

"Great," I said. "Let me review the reason we haven't been discussing your rape. My goal is to teach you how your mind can work for or against you at any given moment. We've discussed the way that your thinking can bring *any* painful event back to life, as if it were happening all over again. You're seeing how this works now. Am I right?"

"Yes," she answered, "I think so."

"Can you give me an example of what I'm talking about so I can see if you're getting it all right?" I asked her.

"I'll try," she said. "Even though my rape was the worst experience of my life, I could just as easily get myself all worked up about the way my little sister spoke down to me the last time we were together."

"Exactly," I responded. "You never, even for one minute, have to pretend that your experience wasn't awful, but you do have some degree of control over the mechanism—your thinking—that brings it back to life."

Robin pointed out to me that despite learning the approach to happiness I was teaching her, thoughts about the event still drifted into her mind. She claimed that it didn't seem as though she had any control over this process. I agreed with her. I told her that this was likely to happen for a long time, if not forever. I reminded her that the goal isn't to get rid of all your negative thoughts, but to develop a different kind of relationship to the ones you have. If you're concerned or frightened each time you have a negative thought, you're going to feel pressure (stress) forever. Since you can't eliminate all your negative thoughts, the only viable solution is to begin to understand that your thoughts don't need to be responded to simply because they happen to exist in your mind. You have a choice. You can react to your thoughts—or you can step back from them and realize that they're just thoughts. They can't hurt you.

To learn the skills to move through therapy quickly, you must see that the way Robin was helped was identical to the way the clients in my earlier examples were helped. We all feel that our individual problems and circumstances are unique. We're right.

But the way to go about feeling better (and less stressed) about these problems is always the same. Our minds are powerful tools, and unfortunately, without an adequate understanding as to how they can trick us, we can be fooled into believing that our circumstances are preventing us from enjoying our lives—and that it's impossible to feel better unless these circumstances are altered.

I began this chapter by suggesting that gratitude is the antidote to virtually all stress, unhappiness, and frustration. I'll end by repeating that suggestion. Life is a gift. You can learn to be grateful that you have dishes to wash rather than angry that you have to wash them. You can learn to be grateful that you have children rather than upset that you have to get up in the middle of the night to nurse them. You can learn to appreciate your job instead of wishing you had a different one. You can look at all of life with an eye toward gratitude. And when you do, it is glorious!

PRINCIPLE NINE:
Be an Observer of Yourself

Knowledge is power.

—FRANCIS BACON

A central theme in Eastern philosophy is the idea of self-observation or self-reflection. Simply put, this means cultivating the ability to watch yourself in motion. Another way of saying this is a phrase I've used in this book: learning to catch yourself in the act when you're thinking or behaving in self-defeating ways. Self-observation is relatively effortless, but it can pay off by helping you become more self-reliant and more pro-active. As you'll see, it's also an easy way to become more relaxed and to take yourself and your problems a little less seriously. Here's an example.

Rick's Difficult Day—He Knew He Did It to Himself

Rick is riding the bus home from work. In his mind he reviews his difficult day. He is clearly caught up in his thinking, and feels overwhelmed. Suddenly, however, Rick realizes he's caught up. What's more, he has learned that the fact that he's caught up in his thinking is far more relevant to the way he currently feels than are the details of what he's caught up in.

With this understanding, he takes a few deep breaths and begins to relax. His sense of relaxation allows him to feel that he's taking a step back from the situation, is slightly removed from it rather than immersed in it. He observes his own thoughts about his day. He sees himself thinking in negative and self-defeating ways: "I hate my job," "No one appreciates me," "I'm getting nowhere," and "I'm going to quit." Since he knows that his being caught up in his thinking is more important than the specific details, he dismisses his negative thoughts from his mind—and begins to feel better. After a while, he feels relieved that it's only his thoughts he has to be concerned with—and that his life isn't as bad as he was just about to convince himself it was.

Anytime you can be aware of and witness your own thoughts, instead of becoming lost or absorbed in them, you're in a position to grow from your experience rather than being immobilized by it. In this example, Rick was able to *see* what he was doing to himself (thinking his way into the emotional doldrums and into a pessimistic state of mind), so he was able to stop.

As simple as this seems (and it is simple), Rick would have been a complete victim of his own negative thoughts and the way they were going to make him feel had it not been for his understanding of this process. If he were like most people, he would have believed that it was his job, and not his thinking, that was responsible for the way he was feeling, and might have spent his evening thinking about the external changes he would have to make to feel better.

Had Rick entertained his thoughts about how bad his day was and how much he disliked his job, he might have ended up on a therapist's couch, only to have the therapist encourage him to think about and discuss how much he disliked his job and his life. After all, the therapist might have argued, "It's important to be honest about your feelings." And of course the therapist would be right. But honesty is a very relative term. It's important to be able to determine accurately whether you're being honest from a place of wisdom and inner peace—or whether you're simply paying attention to stray pessimistic thoughts that stem from a negative state of mind or an extremely low mood. If your thoughts are coming from wisdom, listen to them and act. But if your thoughts are bombarding you with negativity, filling up your mind with pessimism, then simply observe yourself as Rick did and see how easy it is to begin to feel better.

Self-observation and self-reflection become possible only when you're in touch with the idea that *you* are in charge of the thoughts you're thinking, and thus are able to take them a little less seriously.

To give you an even better idea as to why self-observation can be so helpful, let's compare what Rick did, to what another might have done in a similar situation, but without Rick's knowledge.

David's Difficult Day—He Didn't Know He Did It to Himself

Let's assume that David had a similar type day as Rick. He too, was caught up in his thinking, riding the bus on his way home from work. In fact, David's thoughts were identical to Rick's—"I hate my job," "No one appreciates me," "I'm getting nowhere," and "I'm going to quit."

David, however, hadn't cultivated a sense of self-observation. Instead, he had been told that the best way to deal with his negative feelings was to acknowledge and work through them. As he was riding the bus, feeling frustrated, he made a point of acknowledging his feelings. "I feel terrible," he thought to himself! He then continued to think about his predicament, trying to sort things out. He became absorbed and immersed in his negative feelings and seriously wondered if he should quit his job.

The basic difference between these two men can be summarized as follows: David felt that his job was creating his stress, whereas Rick knew that his stress was being created by his own thinking. David also felt that the way out of negative feelings was to work with them, do battle with them. His was the common predicament that we discussed earlier. Whenever you believe your stress comes from something outside yourself, you must then provide a solution that exists outside yourself. In David's case, since he believed his job was creating his negative feelings, he then came up with a solution like quitting his job. Rick, on the other hand, knew that his ill feelings were created within his own mind, therefore the solution was far simpler: When you see yourself thinking in self-defeating ways, you then dismiss those thoughts from your mind.

Rick's strategy is far simpler and more reliable than David's because nothing has to change in order to Rick to feel better. Instead of thinking through his unhappiness, Rick observes himself thinking thoughts of unhappiness—without getting lost in the details of what those thoughts happen to be. This observation enables Rick to "step back" for a moment to see what he is doing to himself—which is thinking his way into a negative state of mind. Once Rick sees that it is himself, and not his job that is creating his negative feelings, he is able to clear his mind and go on with his day.

It would be extremely difficult, if not impossible, for David to stop thinking about his troubles, not because his mind is inferior to Rick's, or that his life is any more difficult, but simply because rather than observing his thoughts as Rick has learned to do, David loses himself in the content of his thoughts, and believes that the object of his thoughts, i.e., his job, are creating his stress. It's the difference between banging your head against a wall and knowing it's you doing the banging—and banging your head against the wall and blaming the wall for your pain. In the first case, you could easily stop the process, because you have control over your own actions; in the second, you would have to wait for the wall to stop hitting you, which of course is impossible.

In chapter 1, I discussed the notion of taking responsibility for your own happiness—and your own unhappiness. I called this process being pro-active. What could be more pro-active than becoming aware of the thoughts that create uneasy feelings within you? When you begin the process of self-observation you take an important step toward pro-activity. You're acknowledging that when *you* are upset, *you* are the one who thinks in a way that's sure to upset you. Self-reflection allows you to witness yourself thinking the thoughts that upset you.

The benefits of self-observation are impressive when it comes to personal growth. It allows you to take full responsibility for the way you're feeling and responding. Once you take responsibility, of course, you can begin to make any necessary changes in your life. If you don't take responsibility, it's tempting to continue blaming others for the way you feel and for the circumstances of your life. Self-observation also allows you to develop and maintain a broader perspective by helping you feel a step removed from many of the dramas of life.

Mary's Story—She Got Caught Up in Her Friends' Problems

Mary was a client who was in the habit of taking on her friends' problems as if they were her own. She would get so caught up in their various difficulties that she could think of almost nothing else. If Janice was having trouble with her husband, for example, Mary would take the problem to heart as if it concerned her own marriage. She would obsess about Janice and her husband, try to come up with solutions, keep herself awake at night because of it. At any time, Mary might be absorbed by twenty separate dramas like Janice's marriage.

Self-observation proved very helpful to Mary. She learned

that feeling stressed was a tipoff that she was caught up in her own thoughts. Before learning the art of self-observation, Mary would respond to her feelings of stress by thinking frantically about her friends' problems. "Maybe there's something I can do," she would think, and her mind would spin furiously onward. Learning self-observation, however, provided a speed bump of sorts in Mary's thinking. Rather than turning up the velocity of her thoughts when she began feeling stressed, as she was used to doing, she learned to pause for a few moments before continuing to think. As she collected herself, she would regain her emotional bearings and begin to watch her thoughts beginning to form.

The act of consciously watching your own thoughts forming slows down their formation to the point that you can see what you are doing to yourself. In Mary's case, here's how it would work: She would, for example, hang up the phone after talking to a friend about her friend's leaking roof. Instantly, she would fall into her typical pattern of dwelling on her friends' problem and begin to feel stressed.

She learned, however, to pay close attention to her stress. "What does this stressful feeling tell me?" she would ask herself. She soon realized that her feeling of stress was *always* trying to tell her the same thing: "I'm too caught up in this." Once she leaped this hurdle, she began to witness her own thoughts. "Oh," she would think to herself, "here I go again beginning to obsess about the leak in Lena's roof."

It wasn't too long before Mary stopped obsessing about her friends altogether. Her growth was significant after she realized the important distinction between a belief that her friends' unsolved problems were causing her to feel upset and stressed and the truth that her own thoughts about her friends' problems were the actual cause of her stress. As she watched herself getting caught up in her thoughts, she began to see how silly it is (her words) to create your own inner turmoil.

Mary isn't any different from the rest of us. We all get caught up in our own thoughts from time to time—it's only the specific details that change from person to person. If you can learn that a feeling of stress is your tipoff that it's time for some self-observation, you'll be preparing yourself for a quick improvement in the quality of your life.

Watch Your Thoughts Like a Movie

When you watch a movie, you're aware that you are separate from what's happening on the screen.

Learning to watch your own thoughts works in a similar manner, developing from your understanding of the role thought plays in your life. You create some distance between yourself and your thoughts, and this sense of distance allows you to watch your thoughts in the same way you might watch a movie.

Watching your own thoughts can be a very entertaining thing to do—even when the content of your thoughts is unpleasant. The distance you create when you watch your thoughts protects you from any negative effects.

It Only Gets Easier

The key to getting better at self-observation is to begin catching yourself in the act of thinking earlier and earlier. In other words, begin to notice that you're off track before you're completely derailed.

As I've explained, stress can be your tipoff—your warning signal that you're caught up in your own mind. The next step is simply to notice and acknowledge that your mind is thinking stressful thoughts, and then *gently* begin to take your attention off whatever you're thinking about. (Don't try too hard—that will only increase your stress.) You'll feel an almost instant shift, a lessening of stress, as you ease off your thinking.

With practice, you'll begin to notice earlier any potential problem—before your thinking gets out of hand and causes you harm. Eventually you'll be able to catch yourself *about to* get caught up in your thinking.

Why Self-Observation Is a Shortcut

> *When you practice self-observation, you cease to blame anyone for anything that isn't working in your life.*

In long-term traditional therapy, the therapist may examine each specific negative feeling you experience as if it had a life of its own, as if examining and analyzing would make it disappear. This process is inconsistent with self-observation for this reason: You notice you're thinking about something, so you think about it some more. You make connections between other thoughts you have about the subject and analyze the specific details of your thoughts. If you're feeling jealous, you wonder why you're feeling jealous. You think some more. You wonder what other factors play a part in your jealous feelings—your spouse, your past, your genes. If you're having angry feelings, you wonder what is making you angry; if you're having frustrated feelings, you wonder why you're frustrated, and so forth.

Self-observation is a shortcut through therapy because all negative feelings are essentially treated equally. Whenever you have a feeling you don't like, it tells you one thing: You're caught up in your own thoughts and it's time to take a step back. As you observe yourself thinking in a negative way, you ease off your thinking in order to feel better and gain deeper perspective and wisdom.

Self-observation is a shortcut because the explanation for the way you're feeling always emphasizes you—always. When you practice self-observation, you become committed to the idea that if you're feeling bad, it's because *you* are creating some type of negative thought that you take too seriously.

> **It's critical to remember that self-observation isn't a prescription for denial.**

You don't practice self-observation in order to pretend you aren't feeling sad, depressed, jealous, or angry. You use it as a tool that can redirect your attention and create a more desirable feeling whenever you choose, and you use it to gain fuller access to your wisdom and common sense. Once you're operating from a place of wisdom and internal equilibrium, you'll know where your negative feelings are coming from. If you're angry and need to take action, you'll take it. If you're depressed about something you have some control over, you'll act. The major difference, when you practice self-observation and gain access to a state of wisdom, will be that your negative feelings won't overwhelm you. You'll be able to maintain your perspective, even in difficult situations.

If you're looking for a way to moderate your feelings, a way to keep yourself from feeling overwhelmed, a way to feel contentment a great deal of the time, the habit of self-observation is the way to go. In conjunction with the other principles in this book, self-observation is a powerful tool for overcoming unhappiness.

PRINCIPLE TEN:
It's Okay Not to Be Perfect

To err is human, to forgive divine.

—ALEXANDER POPE

At first glance, the title of this final chapter might seem a little defeating, if not contradictory to the overall message of this book. Upon closer examination, however, you'll discover that just the opposite is true. Surrendering to the fact that we're all less than perfect, and understanding that the goal of life need not be perfection, but rather happiness and contentment, constitute an important discovery. In fact, freeing yourself from the confines of self-induced perfection is one of the most important shortcuts through therapy. You can learn that life doesn't have to be *any* certain way for you to enjoy it and its many challenges.

The goal of life need not be perfection, but rather happiness and contentment.

There are two important factors to consider here: (1) the circumstances of your life, and (2) how you respond to those

circumstances. Of course you know that at times you have little, if any, control over what happens, but if you understand
the shortcuts to mental health, as I hope you're beginning to
do, you begin to see that you have enormous control over
what you make of what happens in your life.

The single message I want to convey in this chapter is this:
*There is no relationship carved in stone between things being other
than the way you would like them to be and any unhappiness you attach to those conditions.* In other words, it's really okay that your
life isn't perfect—you can still be happy and enjoy it. And you
can be happy without jeopardizing your problem-solving ability or your attention to life's real concerns.

Beth and Arielle

Both Beth and Arielle are driving home after a session with
their respective therapists. Each has spent the past hour discussing the fact that her older sibling received more positive
attention than she did while they were growing up. Both Beth
and Arielle are thirty-five years old, married with two children,
and along with their husbands are struggling to make ends
meet. Both have very ordinary, imperfect lives.

Beth believes that circumstances make a person. She believes that to be happy, a person must "sort out" problems, understand their roots, and dig deep into the "dark side," and in
short, she believes she must be perfect. She thinks about what
she and her therapist discussed. "It wasn't fair," she says to
herself. "The reason I feel so insecure about myself is clearly
related to how little positive praise I received as a child. My
therapist is right. This is a deep-seated problem." Her spirits
drop and she begins to feel pessimistic. Her negativity encourages her to think even more negatively—she spirals downward
toward depression and resentment.

When Beth arrives home she is discouraged. She picks up
the phone and calls her therapist to make another appointment. Her therapist assures her that doing so was a good idea

and an important step toward healing her "inner child." Her therapist insists that Beth is finally being true to her "real" feelings.

Arielle, on the other hand, understands that circumstances don't make a person, they reveal her. She is learning that while it's certainly true that "stuff happens," the critical issue is what you make of that stuff. Arielle understands the important relationship between her thinking and the way she feels. She knows that as she thinks, she will feel the effects of her thoughts just as surely as she will see light when the sun comes up in the morning. Her therapist has taught her to make a game out of catching herself thinking about things that are going to upset her.

Arielle, like Beth, begins to think about her discussion with her therapist as she drives home from her appointment. "My older sister was treated better than I was. It doesn't seem fair." Like Beth, Arielle begins to feel the negative effects of her thinking. All of a sudden, however, Arielle remembers the game her therapist taught her. "Wow," she thinks, "there I go again. It's amazing how I can allow my thinking to run away like that, how I pull myself away from the present moment. I wonder how often I do that to myself." Arielle feels uplifted because she's beginning to believe that there's an end in sight to her therapy. She's starting to understand the dynamics of happiness. Once she's able to catch herself regularly, she will have achieved her goal.

Clearly neither Beth nor Arielle has a perfect life. Both had a less than perfect childhood and both have current troubles as well. The difference between Beth and Arielle can be explained easily. Beth believes that the specific details of what happened are relevant and important to her ability to be happy today. In all likelihood, she will be analyzing the specifics of her childhood for a very long time. She feels that everything needs to be sorted out—bringing her closer to "perfection." The list of possible topics of discussion is virtually unlimited, and with each new issue there will be hundreds of tiny details to ponder. Beth doesn't understand that her thinking plays a critical role in the feelings she is experiencing. She is attempting to analyze her imperfect life without realizing that the analysis itself, not the imperfect life, is creating the very feelings she claims she's trying to rid herself of. In a real sense, she's trapped within the confines of her own thinking without realizing that the trap is being created from moment to moment through her own thoughts.

Arielle, on the other hand, has learned that sorting out the details is an endless and usually frustrating experience that ultimately doesn't change anything or make her feel any better. This doesn't mean that the details of her life aren't important to her—they most certainly are. Rather than dig deep for specifics, however, she has learned to search for the principles most likely to help her feel better today. Certainly Arielle isn't superior to or any more capable of happiness than Beth, but she has learned a few simple tools that Beth hasn't. She has discovered that she is the navigator of her own ship; she is writing the script for her own life from moment to moment. She understands the important relationship between her thinking and her feelings. She has learned to detect her negative feelings as they come up—and sometimes she can even detect their coming on before they arrive. Rather than studying the specifics of her negative feelings and attempting to label them, as Beth tends to do, she uses her feelings as a tool to let her know whether or not she's functioning at her best. When she isn't, she tries to make a gentle mental adjustment, bringing her attention back to the here and now. Perhaps most important, she understands that she doesn't have to be perfect to be happy.

Arielle is in an excellent position regarding her emotional health and potential happiness because regardless of what she happens to be thinking about, or what experiences she's going through, she always knows how to prevent herself from dropping into a state of extended fear, anger, or depression. She takes absolute control of her life by understanding that when she feels bad, it's because she's taking her own thoughts too seriously. Her understanding is generic, meaning it applies to whatever she happens to be going through.

Unfortunately, Beth is in a very difficult position. She believes that she has little, if any, control over the way she feels because the source of her feelings is external. For example, she believes that her parents are responsible for her current set of negative feelings because they didn't give her the positive attention she so desperately needed. There's really no way out of this negative loop for Beth. She can't change anything that happened to her in childhood. Each and every time she thinks about what happened, she will experience negative feelings, because rather than seeing her feelings as an indicator that lets her know whether or not she's on track, she views her feelings as coming from external sources.

Whereas Arielle's understanding is generic, meaning it will help her regardless of what she's going through, Beth's beliefs are case-specific, meaning each new issue will have to be thought through individually. So, even if Beth eventually does work through her feelings regarding her parents, the next time she remembers a painful event from her past or experiences a difficulty in the present, she'll be starting over. Nothing in her consciousness has shifted to the point that it will help her on a continuing basis.

One of the reasons that Arielle can discuss and learn from her mistakes and problems is that she understands that *there is no reason good enough to cause unhappiness!* She doesn't have to be perfect! Happiness is independent of the circumstances of life. If the issue weren't her childhood, but her relationship to her husband, Arielle would respond in a similar manner. She would be able to discuss her issues, learn from them, have thoughts about them, but not be immobilized by them. Why? Because she puts her happiness first. She understands that it's okay not to be perfect. She knows that this isn't a statement about her self-worth, but a truism that everyone must accept. No one is perfect and no one's life is perfect. So what? This doesn't mean she shouldn't strive to be her best, even work toward perfection, but she need not attach her happiness to this elusive goal.

Beth has attached a condition to her happiness. She believes she must work through the issues of her childhood to be happy today. To her this means thinking about the most painful parts of her early life and searching for connections between those painful events and her current problems and feelings. As thoughts enter her mind regarding her childhood, she assumes they must be there for an important reason. She then studies her thoughts with her therapist (or by herself) and arrives at some conclusion.

One problem Beth faces is a common obstacle for many people who enter therapy. Let's assume for a moment that she does work through her childhood issues to her satisfaction. What's going to happen to her the next time she drops into a low mood and has a negative series of thoughts about her childhood? In all likelihood, the process will start again.

Please understand that I'm *not* suggesting that it's inappropriate or unimportant to understand the roots of your psychological patterns, or to take a close look at the impact your childhood had on your present life. That is an entirely different subject, something you and your therapist might want to discuss. I'm simply familiarizing you with those mental processes that take you away from where you want to be—happy and content. If you're curious about your childhood, terrific. If you thirst for knowledge regarding your patterns or tendencies, wonderful. What I'm discussing in this book isn't that it's wrong or worthless to study these things, but the effect these practices will have on the way you feel.

Once you understand the relationship between your thoughts and your feelings, you're protected from the ill effects of your own thinking. As long as you know it's you who creates your negative feelings and not the events and circumstances around you, you'll be okay. You'll be able to direct your own life, and you'll be able to tell your therapist when you've had enough.

Life is not a dress rehearsal for some later date.

Life is what is happening right now, at this very moment. All the rest—the past and future—are alive only in your thinking. This being the case, what could possibly be more important than learning the skills needed to feel good on a continuing basis?

It's not only possible but practical to allow yourself the privilege of feeling good, even if your life isn't perfect. It all starts with the decision that your life and the way you feel are too important to take too seriously. Noncontingent positive feeling, or feeling good without conditions, involves understanding the important role your thinking plays in the way you feel from moment to moment. It involves the recognition of when and how you need to make adjustments in your thinking.

Your Feelings—Go with the Flow

When you're feeling good, secure, motivated, content—when you feel gratitude for the gift of life, you're on track. You're obviously using your ability to think in a constructive way. No mental adjustments need to be considered. If, however, you're feeling insecure, angry, hostile, frightened, pessimistic, depressed, or in some other way immobilized, you're being given the internal message that you're using your own thinking against yourself. Your thoughts are taking you away from where you want to be—happy.

Whenever you're feeling negative or low, you've approached an important crossroads. One direction takes you toward the reason you're upset, toward specifics and details. It encourages examination and analysis. This direction works on the assumption that "I'm not okay and that's *not* okay." It's not okay simply to feel bad—you must come up with an explanation as to why you feel bad and then do something to make yourself feel better. This is the direction most people take. It's the direction most therapists take. It's the wrong direction to take if your goal is to feel better.

If you think back to the discussion of moods, you'll recall that feeling bad, or dropping into a low mood or state of mind, is a natural part of life. Luckily, feeling good, or experiencing a higher mood or state of mind, is also natural. A natural flow or rhythm exists between these higher and lower moods.

When you're feeling down and that's not okay with you, you end up suffering, fighting a battle with yourself. Sometimes you're simply down and there's no reason for it except that you're down. When you (or your therapist) try to come up with reasons for the way you're feeling, you're setting a trap for yourself that's difficult to break free of. The more you think in a low state of mind, the worse you'll feel because your thoughts create additional feelings to contend with. You end up convincing yourself that you really do have good reason to feel bad. When a therapist asks you to explain what you're feeling, often what he or she is really asking you to do is explain how you see life during those moments when your mood is low.

If you can simply allow yourself to be down and let it be okay, doing nothing about it, knowing that "this too shall pass," it will. No explanation will be needed, no analysis, nothing. Just the understanding that it's okay not to be perfect. This quiet acceptance of or surrender to the natural flow of life allows your mind the space to be free. It opens the door to feeling good again.

The Process and the Goal Are One and the Same

There is no way to happiness—happiness is the way. The process and the goal are one and the same. In other words, when you learn to find access to a more contented feeling you realize that this feeling isn't leading somewhere else—it's all you've been looking for. And this feeling can be called up virtually anytime once you understand the dynamics of happiness.

Throughout this book I have discussed the dynamics of happiness and the dynamics of unhappiness—what makes you tick and what makes you fall apart. You've seen that these dynamics are the same regardless of your individual circumstances. In other words, whether you're dealing with a financial crisis, a difficult marriage, a career concern, general anxiety, ill health, even a tragedy, the determining factor that will ultimately decide how you get through the crisis isn't the severity of the crisis, but the way you relate to it.

In no way does this minimize the difficulty of the circumstances you face in your life. I'm not telling you that life is always easy or that if you implement the principles you've learned in this book you'll walk around with a silly grin on your face when times are tough. What I do say is that your personal happiness can, and does, exist independent of what's going on around you—that is, if you learn not to exacerbate the problems in your life with your own thinking, but learn to relate to your thinking in a healthier way.

You can learn to minimize the damage you inflict on yourself by learning to detect your dysfunctional thinking earlier and earlier. You'll learn to pay attention to the way you're feeling and then use your feelings, even the negative ones, to alert you when you come to an important crossroads—when you are about to spiral downward toward the emotional doldrums. You can suspend trust in your thoughts when you aren't feeling well—physically or emotionally. Low moods are deceptive and seductive, and lead to a sense of urgency.

You can minimize your emotional pain by an understanding of the principle of separate realities—the idea that we each see a different world and are each convinced that our version is the right one.

Trust your wisdom more than your thinking by remembering that wisdom, by definition, is more trustworthy than your habitual thoughts. Your wisdom, or common sense, exists outside the confines of your thinking mind. You gain access to it when you quiet down and listen for inspiration or insight. You can add to your contentment by choosing to be happy rather than be right. Being right or making someone else wrong is worthless if it requires energy that could be better spent enjoying your life. Given the choice, let someone else be right for a change. Choose your battles carefully and allow yourself the luxury of feeling happy.

These mental dynamics, along with the others I've discussed, are the real factors that determine whether or not you're going to enjoy your life—or struggle against it. It may always seem as though your life needs to be rearranged in some way so that you can be happy. But don't fall into this trap. Give yourself permission and strive to feel happy first. Out of that happier place, your life will get better.

Your Happiness Isn't Tied to Your Dreams

> *There is an enormous difference between having a dream and making your happiness conditional on your dream's coming true.*

I like to think in terms of pipe dreams. These are your personal dreams, desires, and goals, which may or may not come true. You'd really like them to come true—but your happiness isn't tied to them.

I have had a pipe dream, for example, of moving to Hawaii for a year with my wife and our two children. I dream of living close to the beach, writing a book, and spending most of my time with the kids. For many reasons, however, including my work and travel schedule, my wife's preferences, and the kids' schools and friends, it has been unrealistic for us to make this move. I'm not giving up on my pipe dream, however, because I believe this is something I can make happen. I think it would be a marvelous experience for me and my family. The dream continues.

My happiness, however, isn't tied to whether or not this ever actually happens—not even one percent. The truth is, it might not happen. The more important truth is, it doesn't really matter.

I could turn this simple pipe dream into a major source of unhappiness if I thought about how much I want to move to Hawaii, gave significance to these thoughts, and believed them important. I could compound the problem by thinking about my dream and how it isn't coming true when I'm in a low mood. In fact, this has happened to me on many occasions. My mood dropped. I began feeling sorry for myself. A few thoughts about my pipe dream entered my mind—and the fork in the road presented itself. I then had to make the choice to trust my thinking or realize that I was in another low mood and it wasn't really an emergency after all.

Most but not all of the time, I realize it quickly when I'm in a low mood. This recognition saves me from torturing myself with my own thinking. I usually remember that in higher states of mind, this identical issue is seen as a pipe dream, whereas right now, it seems like a big deal.

The dynamics of unhappiness apply whether your pipe dream is finding the ideal mate, getting a deserved promotion, winning the lottery, or being able to afford a new car. It doesn't matter what issue you're dealing with. If you attach your happiness to something external to yourself, you'll spend most of your life waiting to be happy. It doesn't have to be this way.

Most of what you read and most of what you hear from "experts" will attempt to convince you that the opposite is true. You'll be told that it's important to analyze, discuss, and think about what's wrong so that you'll be honest about your feelings. The unspoken message is: You're not okay—and that's not okay! Advocates of this philosophy will insist that for you to be happy, your pipe dreams must come true. They'll ask you, "How can you be happy if you're not getting what you want from life?" As absurd as it may seem, I have been accused in public by a respected mental-health worker of being in denial for choosing to be happy before my pipe dream of living in Hawaii ever comes true. He claimed I wasn't being honest about my true feelings.

If you understand what you've read in this book, you'll get what you want from life—happiness. You'll live from moment to moment, with an understanding of the dynamics of happiness and the dynamics of unhappiness. You'll understand the mental processes you engage in that pull you away from happiness. You'll know what techniques to use to point yourself toward happiness again.

Of course you want life to run smoothly, and of course you want circumstances to turn in your favor—but they absolutely don't have to. By understanding the dynamics of happiness, you can turn all of your life into the marvelous adventure that it really is. Perhaps as important as any message in this book is the motto: It's okay not to be perfect!